# Dedicated to

*My parents*

*Kashmira & Kandarp Trivedi*

For always believing in me, encouraging me and inspiring me to reach for my dreams.

Your unwavering support and love have shaped who I am today and for that,

I am forever grateful.

# GRATITUDE

First and foremost, my deepest thanks go to God for the blessings of insight and guidance on this journey. This book is a piece of my heart, and I owe its inspiration to divine grace.

To my parents—you have always believed in me, nurtured my dreams, and been my unwavering support system. Thank you for everything. To my brother, Yash Trivedi, your encouragement has meant more to me than you know. And to my husband, Ashutosh Abhyankar, and my mother-in-law, Jyotsna Abhyankar—thank you for your endless patience, love, and understanding. Your support has given me the freedom to pour myself fully into this project.

I'm especially grateful to my mentors, Dr. Sandeep Kelkar and Dr. Raakesh Kriplani. Your wisdom, guidance, and unwavering support have been a cornerstone of this work, and I'm so lucky to have learned from you.

A heartfelt thank you to Dr. Devanshi Jhalani, Dr. Kiran Tiwari, Dr. Afreen Chunawala, and Shruti Ambikar, who offered thoughtful feedback from a parent's perspective. Your insights have truly enriched this book, making it something I hope will resonate deeply with parents everywhere.

To Rtn. Deepak Chawla—thank you for your invaluable guidance and encouragement. And to Dr. Anju Kapoor, thank you for honouring this book with your foreword; it brings a depth and warmth that I cherish.

A special thanks to Hemangi Tai for your generous help with the legal details, making sure everything was handled with care.

To my dear friends—thank you for your laughter, companionship, and endless encouragement. You've reminded me time and again of the power of friendship, and I'm grateful beyond words.

This book is truly a labour of love, enriched by the insights, kindness, and inspiration of so many wonderful people. Thank you all for being such an important part of this journey with me.

# CONTENTS


*Foreword*...................................................................9
*Introduction* ...........................................................11

Chapter 1    Babies Need Humans, Not Screens!...................17

Chapter 2    What AI Now and Later Means for
0-5-Year-Olds: Using AI Well, Wisely,
and Safely....................................................35

Chapter 3    Identifying Signs of Higher Digital
Dependency or Addiction in Your Child ........45

Chapter 4    Ideal Screen Time Limits...............................49

Chapter 5    Walk the Talk ...........................................51

Chapter 6    Parenting Styles and Internet Addiction..........75

Chapter 7    Practical Problems Faced By Working
Parents and Their Possible Solutions...............81

Chapter 8    Handling Peer Pressure ...............................89

Chapter 9    Steps to Take If Your Child Is Already
Dependent on Screens ..................................93

Chapter 10   Early Childhood Device Use
Assessment (EC-DUA) .................................97

Chapter 11   Internet Addiction Test for Adults................. 107

Chapter 12   Cultivating Balance for a Digital Future........ 111

*Summary Tables* ................................................ 113

# FOREWORD

In an era where digital screens are a constant presence, a book that emphasizes the importance of digital well-being for future generations is both timely and essential. Dr. Kruti Trivedi Abhyankar has created an insightful guide that navigates the unique challenges of parenting in the digital age, presenting readers with a thoughtful perspective on raising children amidst the many screens that fill our world.

In today's fast-paced, technology-driven world, setting mindful screen-time limits for children has become a crucial aspect of parenting. With devices at every turn, managing digital habits is more than a daily task—it's a commitment to nurturing balanced, healthy growth in our children. While digital tools offer many benefits, they also bring the potential for dependency and even addiction, especially in younger children. Dr. Abhyankar's approach highlights the need for awareness and proactive guidance in protecting children from these risks.

The importance of direct human interaction, particularly in a child's early years, cannot be overstated. Babies and toddlers flourish through engagement with caregivers and their surroundings. Screens cannot substitute the vital developmental experiences that come from bonding and playing with loved ones. This truth emphasizes the need for parents to prioritize human connection over digital distractions, fostering an environment where children feel seen, heard, and deeply connected.

As a practicing psychologist, I have witnessed the profound impact of excessive screen exposure on children's mental, emotional, and social development. I've seen the challenges families face in balancing technology use with authentic, face-to-face interactions. Without careful management, screen time can interfere with a child's natural growth and hinder their ability to form lasting, real-world connections.

As caregivers, we hold a unique responsibility to instill screen discipline within our families. While this journey may be challenging, it's also empowering. By setting thoughtful boundaries, we can foster healthier relationships with technology that will benefit our children throughout their lives. My mentors once reminded me that parenting is a lifelong commitment, and that there are no problem children—only problem parents.

For young parents, I strongly encourage you to read through to the end of this book. Dr. Abhyankar shares practical, invaluable tips that will not only make you more effective parents but also empower you to play a vital role in enriching your children's lives.

**– Dr Anju Kapoor**
Principal, SVKM's UPG College of Arts,
Science and Commerce.
Practicing Psychologist & therapist.

# INTRODUCTION

Once, on my way to conduct an awareness session about Digital well-being for college students in Ghatkopar, Mumbai, I had an unexpected encounter on the train. I found a cozy spot by the window in the ladies' compartment from Thane and started enjoying the passing scenery. However, my peaceful moment was soon interrupted by the loud cries of a 4-year-old boy sitting with his mother. As the minutes passed and the cries continued, I couldn't help but wonder what was causing the distress. I turned to the boy's mother and asked why he was so upset. Her face told a story of embarrassment, frustration, and exhaustion as she explained, "He wants my phone to play games, but I won't give it to him." At that moment, I realized many parents struggle to manage their children's screen time.

Parenting in the digital age presents many challenges and opportunities, shaping how children interact with the world around them. As technology rapidly advances, screens have become essential daily, offering endless learning, entertainment, and communication possibilities. However, these benefits also raise concerns about the impact of excessive screen time on children's development and well-being.

This book will explore the complex relationship between children, screens, and parenting styles in today's digital landscape. Drawing on research, practical insights, and real-life experiences, we will delve into the various dimensions of screen use among children aged 0 to 5 years and guide parents in navigating this evolving terrain.

It's essential to understand the impact of screens on children and how it affects them. Exploring how excessive screen time can affect our children, from decreased physical activity to disrupted sleep patterns and delayed social-emotional growth, is truly eye-opening. By recognizing these effects, parents can make thoughtful choices and implement strategies to ensure their kids have a healthy balance when it comes to screen time.

A crucial part of our discussion is the influence of different parenting styles on children's behaviours and attitudes towards screens. Drawing from the valuable insights of psychologists like Diana Baumrind, we will delve into the four main parenting styles—authoritative, authoritarian, permissive/indulgent, and neglectful/uninvolved—and their impact on-screen use.

Additionally, we acknowledge the real challenges that working parents face in managing their children's screen time. Parents encounter numerous hurdles in fostering healthy screen habits, from juggling work responsibilities to navigating peer pressure and societal expectations. Despite these challenges, parents have many opportunities to guide their children towards a positive and balanced relationship with screens. Through actionable strategies and evidence-based recommendations, we empower parents to overcome these challenges and cultivate a positive digital environment for their children.

We offer a roadmap for intervention and support for parents grappling with the reality of a child already dependent on screens. By collecting data, identifying triggers, and implementing gradual changes, parents can guide their children towards healthier screen habits and a more balanced lifestyle.

Ultimately, this book serves as a comprehensive guide for parents seeking to navigate the complexities of parenting in the digital age. With practical insights, evidence-based strategies, and a deep understanding of children's needs, we empower parents to find meaningful connections, promote responsible digital citizenship, and nurture the well-being of their children in an increasingly digital world.

"उद्धरेदात्मनाऽत्मानं नात्मानमवसादयेत्।
आत्मैव ह्यात्मनो बन्धुरात्मैव रिपुरात्मनः॥"

"Let a person lift themselves by their own mind and not degrade themselves. The mind is the friend of the conditioned soul, and the mind is the enemy as well."

– *Bhagavad Gita*, Chapter 6, Verse 5

# Chapter 1

# BABIES NEED HUMANS, NOT SCREENS!

I found a suitable caption for this chapter on a UNICEF parenting page:

"Babies Need Humans, Not Screens!" [18]

Recently, my 5-year-old nephew visited me, clutching an iPad as he entered my home. "Maasi, do you have Wi-Fi at home? Please give me the password; otherwise, I will not be able to play online," he promptly asked. Despite actually having Wi-Fi, I informed him that we did not. I encouraged him to engage with me instead of his iPad. Initially disappointed, he reluctantly agreed. I initiated various activities, from playing games to reading books, and even took him to the garden in our neighbourhood. Surprisingly, he did not reach for his iPad all day, enjoying our interactions. Later, I handed him an activity book when I had tasks. He happily immersed himself in it for hours without once requesting his iPad.

When my sister returned home from work that night, she inquired about his day, and he eagerly recounted our activities. My sister was shocked, remarking, "Kruti, I have rarely seen him so joyful and engaged. Usually, he is glued to his iPad and barely communicates with us. If we attempt to take it away, he throws tantrums until we return it."

I patiently listened to what she said, and once she stopped, I started giving her *gyaan* (as usual) about all the cons of using screens for more than the prescribed time. Whatever I told her, I will provide the same *gyaan* to you all now.

**The effects of excessive screen time on children aged 0 to 5 years as indicated by recent studies**

## a)  Effect on Language and Motor Development

A population-based cross-sectional study was conducted in Tamil Nadu, India's rural and urban health centres. Seven hundred eighteen children (396 rural and 322 urban) were selected and studied. Screen time estimates were obtained from parents/guardians after a 7-day observation period. This study revealed a significant association between increased screen time and developmental delay, particularly affecting language acquisition and communication skills.

Similarly, another study conducted in Chandigarh, a North Indian Union Territory, focused on the prevalence of screen time among 2 to 5 year-old children. This study of 400 randomly selected children highlighted a high prevalence of excessive screen time in this age group. Additionally, it found associations between screen time and factors such as daycare attendance, caregivers' screen time, mothers' educational status, and educational digital content. [1][2]

The studies collectively indicate that higher screen time in children under five years of age leads to developmental delays, particularly in language and communication skills. The lack of interactive human communication during screen time affects language development, contributing to a rise in preschoolers with language delays. Moreover, increased screen time correlates with lower fine motor skills, as evidenced by research published in the Journal of Sport and Health Science. [3]

The passive nature of screen time further exacerbates motor developmental delays by limiting physical activity and free play opportunities. Prolonged screen time restricts movement and engagement in physical activities, which is essential for developing fundamental motor skills.

## b) Effect on Emotional and Social Development

Research indicates that excessive screen time impedes emotional and social development. It impairs young children's ability to read faces and learn social skills, crucial for developing empathy.

Charles Nelson, a Harvard neuroscientist who studies the impact of neglect on children's brains, says, "Until babies develop language, all communication is non-verbal, so they depend heavily on looking at a face and deriving meaning from that face. Is this person happy with me, or are they upset with me?" That two-way interaction between children and adult caregivers is critically important for brain development. [18]

Screen exposure reduces babies' ability to read human emotions and control their frustration. It also detracts from activities that help boost their brain power, like playing and interacting with other children. [18]

## c) Effect on Cognitive Development

Screen exposure detracts from activities that stimulate cognitive development and boost brainpower, such as play and peer interaction. A cross-sectional study in Thiruvalla revealed that preschool children often exceed recommended screen time limits, with inconsistent parental supervision associated with suspected cognitive delays. Cognitive development encompasses acquiring, understanding, organising, and utilising information gathered through sensory experiences. Higher screen time disrupts this process, impeding children's overall development.

In summary, excessive screen time adversely affects children's development, including motor skills, learning, emotional and social development, and cognitive development. Limiting screen time and promoting meaningful human interaction and engaging activities are essential for supporting healthy child development.

## d)  Virtual Autism

In recent years, the term "Virtual Autism" has emerged as a concept denoting the manifestation of behaviours akin to those associated with Autism Spectrum Disorder (ASD) due to prolonged exposure to digital screens. Coined by Romanian psychologist Marius Teodor Zamfir in 2018, Virtual Autism highlights the potential consequences of excessive screen time, particularly for children under three.

Zamfir proposed that when young children spend more than four hours a day immersed in digital media, they may experience "sensory-motor and socio-affective deprivation." This phenomenon underscores a critical concern regarding the impact of modern technology on child development. Some studies suggest increased screen time is associated with changes in melanopsin-expressing neurons and decreased gamma-aminobutyric acid (GABA) neurotransmitter. These physiological changes may result in aberrant behaviour, decreased cognitive function, and impaired language development.

While individuals with ASD contend with genuine challenges in social communication and interaction, Virtual Autism represents a distinct set of behaviours induced or exacerbated by extensive engagement with digital technologies.

A recent study conducted on 60 children exhibiting autistic symptoms shed light on the effects of in-depth screen exposure. Utilising an online examination tool named C-VAT (Checklist for Virtual Autism), researchers aimed to discern the typical developmental patterns of children and investigate deviations caused by rigorous screen exposure. The findings were illuminating: children subjected to extensive screen time demonstrated traits akin to autism, termed "Virtual Autism". These children exhibited marked improvement when screen duration was reduced to zero, underscoring the potential reversibility of Virtual Autism through intervention strategies.

Moreover, it is essential to differentiate between Virtual Autism and ASD, as the former arises as a response to virtual stimuli. At the same time, the latter encompasses inherent challenges in social interaction and communication. Virtual Autism, induced by prolonged exposure to digital environments, represents a distinct condition that warrants attention and intervention. [4][5][6]

## e) Effect on Learning

Moving on to the effect on learning, Patricia Kuhl, a prominent brain scientist, highlights the limited effectiveness of machines in facilitating learning for infants. Despite the allure of captivating videos, infants under a year old do not effectively learn from screens. Kuhl emphasises the unparalleled benefits of human interaction in promoting optimal learning outcomes, stressing that babies require interaction with live human beings for meaningful learning experiences. [7]

## f) Effect on Sleep

The impact of excessive screen time on sleep quality and quantity is a significant concern, especially among preschool-aged children. According to data from US population-based studies, approximately 30% of preschool-aged children do not obtain adequate sleep. Numerous observational studies have shown that increased screen time, encompassing television, computers, video games, and mobile devices, is associated with delayed bedtimes and reduced total sleep duration in more than 90% of cases among children and adolescents. [8]

Because of social media ads, almost everyone is aware of blue light. There are ads about blue light filter glasses, screens, apps, and more. So, what is this blue light, and how does it affect the sleep cycle?

One key factor contributing to sleep disturbances associated with screen time is exposure to blue light. Blue light, which is part of the light we can see, i.e., sunlight, affects how awake we feel, the hormones our bodies make, and our sleep patterns.

Circadian rhythm is a natural, internal process that regulates the sleep-wake cycle and repeats roughly every 24 hours. All our cycles are dependent on sunset and sunrise. As stated above, we are exposed to blue light from the sunlight.

Blue light stimulates parts of the brain, signalling that it is daytime and the body needs to be alert and awake. When the sun sets, our body starts preparing for a good night's sleep through the secretion of different hormones and chemicals. Exposure to blue light in the hours leading up to bedtime can hinder sleep. Blue light suppresses the body's release of melatonin, a hormone that makes us feel drowsy. While this promotes wakefulness during the day, it becomes unhelpful at night when trying to sleep. Exposure to blue light in the evening can trick our brain into thinking it is still daytime, disrupting circadian rhythms and leaving us alert instead of tired.

This disruption can lead to various sleep-related issues, including difficulty falling asleep, delayed sleep onset, daytime drowsiness, and irritability, affecting children and adults alike. [19]

## g) Screens and Childhood Obesity

Excessive screen time among children is linked to an increased risk of obesity through indirect mechanisms. The rise in the incidence of childhood obesity from excessive screen time can be attributed to some reasons:

- Lack of physical activity
- Increased incidences of snacking and binge eating of high-calorie, junk, and low-nutrient value food while they are engrossed in their screens.
- More exposure to food advertisements – According to a Harvard University study, food advertisements can increase snacking habits by 45%.
- Lack of sleep can slow down the metabolic rate.

However, interventions to reduce screen time and regulate content consumption have shown promising results. Studies have demonstrated that children who experienced reduced screen time exhibited improvements in sleep duration, behaviour, sociability, academic performance, and weight management. [9]

## h) Effect on Attention Span

The impact of excessive screen time on attention span is multifaceted. Research headed by Michael Manos from the Cleveland Clinic draws the concerning link between prolonged screen exposure and focus-related conditions, particularly among young children. Manos's findings suggest that children under the age of five who spend more than two hours daily on screens are nearly eight times more likely to be diagnosed with Attention Deficit Hyperactivity Disorder (ADHD) or other focus-related issues. The reason behind this correlation lies in screen-based activities, which provide immediate and repeated stimulation. When children become accustomed to such rapid and frequent forms of engagement, they may find focusing on less captivating real-world tasks challenging.

This difficulty in maintaining focus stems from the brain's operation with two distinct types of attention: automatic and directed. Automatic attention is associated with engaging activities like scrolling through social media feeds or playing video games. In contrast, directed attention, required for tasks like studying or reading, is a more deliberate and effortful process. Excessive exposure to screens, which predominantly activate automatic attention, can overshadow the development and utilisation of directed attention. Consequently, children may struggle to engage effectively with essential but less inherently stimulating tasks, impacting their academic performance and overall productivity. [10]

## i)  Effect on Impulse Control

Screen time can affect how well we control our impulses, which is crucial to managing our behaviour. Research shows that spending too much time on screens can change how a chemical called dopamine works in our brains. Dopamine is a chemical that makes us feel good when we do things we enjoy. When we use screens a lot, like playing games or watching videos, our brains release dopamine, making us feel good. But this can also make us want to keep using screens, even when we should stop. It is like how some people feel when they use addictive substances like drugs.

Because screens give us instant rewards, like winning a game or getting likes on social media, our brains expect them, making it hard to control our impulses. Spending too much time on screens can make it challenging for kids to wait for things they want or make good decisions. They might have trouble focusing on schoolwork or chores because they would rather be on their screens.

For example, imagine a parent notices that their child, Raj, spends several hours each day playing video games on his tablet. Raj becomes increasingly irritable when asked to stop playing, often throwing tantrums or refusing to comply. Despite knowing that he has homework to complete or chores to do, Raj struggles to tear himself away from the screen. His parents observe that Raj's impulsive behaviour extends beyond gaming, as he becomes more prone to making rash decisions and has difficulty concentrating on tasks that require delayed gratification, like studying for exams.

In this example, Raj's excessive screen time has negatively impacted his impulse control, making it difficult to manage his behaviour and priorities.

## j)  Effect on Physical Health

### Headache

Many paediatricians have found that high screen time is one of the major causes of headaches in children. Spending too much time staring at a screen, such as a phone, tablet, or computer, can cause digital eyestrain, a key trigger for headaches. When your child cries or complains of recurrent headaches, reflecting on their screen time and disciplining them around their screens will help.

### Eyes and ears

As mentioned above, higher screen time causes digital eyestrain, which triggers headaches and leads to eye redness, dryness, watering, and irritation.

ENT doctors have seen an increase in hearing problems, even in children, due to listening to music at a higher volume for a long time on a smartphone, tablet, or computer. Using in-ear earphones can increase earwax secretion, causing ear blockage and infection. Listening to music at a higher volume for a long time can also cause irritation, a lower attention span, memory issues, and anger.

## Neck and back pain

More children suffer from neck and back problems due to increased screen time on phones, tablets, and other electronic devices. Text neck or tech neck syndrome is a group of symptoms caused by holding or looking at screens with the neck flexed at an angle. Children also sit in poor posture—slouched and using screens—which can give rise to back and posture problems.

According to a 2014 study published in Surgical Technology International, the amount of pressure exerted on the neck increases significantly as we tilt our heads downward. For instance, when looking straight ahead with arms at the sides, the pressure is about 10 to 12 pounds. However, looking down at a 15-degree angle increases this pressure to 27 pounds; at 30 degrees, it reaches 40 pounds. At steeper angles of 45 and 60 degrees, the pressure spikes to 49 and 60 pounds, respectively. Since most of us bend our necks between 20 and 45 degrees when using our phones, this places considerable strain on the spine. [20]

When children spend excessive time on phones at the expense of physical play, it can lead to various health issues such as poor bone health, neck pain, back pain, and shoulder pain. Cordelia Carter, M.D., a paediatric orthopaedic surgeon and director of the Paediatric Sports Medicine Centre at Hassenfeld Children's Hospital, describes "text neck" as an overuse injury resulting from prolonged phone use. Additionally, she refers to the lack of physical playtime as an "underuse injury." The erector muscles lining the spinal column, which support the core, weaken over time if not actively engaged while sitting, highlighting the importance of balancing screen time with physical activity to maintain spinal health and overall well-being.

Poor texting posture can be particularly problematic for young users whose spines are still developing and could lead to arthritic changes in the spine, bone spurs, or muscle deformities. Research findings indicate that kyphosis, an S-curve of the spine or rounded back, can be caused by the loosening of ligaments in the spine aggravated by screen use. [11][12]

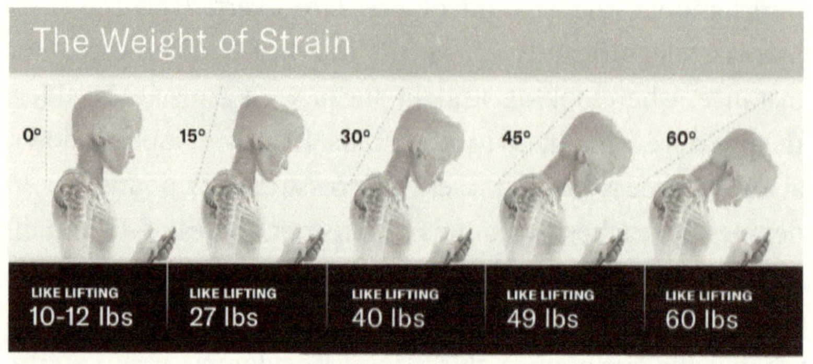


## RSI

Repetitive Strain Injuries (RSI) include bodily injuries from reduced blood flow to muscles, bones, and ligaments due to poor posture or repetitive movements. In children, RSIs can result from the repeated motions typical in video game playing, excessive texting or swiping on smartphones, and prolonged screen use. Examples of RSIs stemming from excessive screen time include tendonitis in the shoulder, elbow, forearm, wrist, or hand, as well as back or neck strain and carpal tunnel syndrome. [12]

## k) Brain Changes Due to Screens

The human brain is remarkably adaptable and responsive to external stimuli, including prolonged screen exposure. As technology becomes increasingly integrated into daily life, concerns about the impact of excessive screen time on brain function have garnered significant attention. Emerging research sheds light on how the brain responds to increased screen time, highlighting both structural and functional changes that may occur.

**Structural Changes**

One notable area of investigation concerns the structural changes within the brain, particularly in regions associated with learning, attention, and communication. A study published in JAMA Paediatrics in 2019 found that preschoolers who spent considerable time on screens exhibited alterations in white matter integrity. White matter, comprised of nerve fibres facilitating communication between brain regions, plays a crucial role in learning and cognitive function. The observed decrease in white matter integrity suggests potential disruptions in neural connectivity, which may impact learning ability and information processing.

Moreover, research led by John Hutton from the Cincinnati Children's Hospital explored the impact of screen-based learning on brain activity. Brain imaging studies comparing children reading animated stories on screens versus traditional picture books revealed notable differences in neural activation patterns. Children engaging with screen-based stories exhibited heightened activity in visual processing regions of the brain, while areas associated with language and imagination showed decreased engagement. This imbalance in neural activation suggests that hyper-engagement with visual stimuli on screens may come at the expense of internally generated imagination and language development. [13][14]

**Functional Changes**

In addition to structural alterations, increased screen time can also influence the functional connectivity of the brain, affecting attention, decision-making, and emotional regulation. A study published in PLOS ONE examined brain scans of individuals diagnosed with Internet Addiction Disorder (IAD) and found patterns of abnormal white matter compared to non-addicted individuals. These changes were observed in regions implicated in emotional processing, decision-making, and impulse control, suggesting potential disruptions in neural pathways associated with addictive behaviours.

The impact of cell phone radiation on children has been a topic of concern and scientific investigation for years. Several studies have highlighted potential risks associated with prolonged exposure to radiofrequency (RF) energy emitted by cell phones, particularly in the context of children's developing brains and bodies. [15][16]

## 1)  Effect of Radiation

1. **Increased Exposure in Children:** A 2010 study has shown that children are more susceptible to RF radiation due to their proportionally smaller heads and brains than adults. Despite this anatomical difference, children receive similar levels of cell phone radiation as adults, leading to higher RF energy deposition in their brain regions. The American Academy of Paediatrics

corroborates these findings, noting that RF energy deposition is significantly higher in children's brains and bone marrow than in adults when using mobile phones. Heightened exposure raises concerns about the potential long-term effects of RF radiation on children's health.

2. **Elevated Risk of Brain Tumours:** Research has also suggested a correlation between early cell phone use and an increased risk of developing brain tumours, particularly among individuals who use wireless phones before age 20. Due to children's thinner tissues and bones, the radiation source to the brain is closer, potentially amplifying the risk of adverse health outcomes. While the exact mechanisms underlying this association require further investigation, the findings emphasise the importance of caution regarding children's cell phone usage. [21]

3. **Behavioural Implications:** Beyond physiological concerns, studies have explored the potential impact of cell phone exposure on children's behaviour. Research suggests that children exposed to cell phone radiation during pregnancy or early childhood may be at a heightened risk of developing behavioural problems, including hyperactivity and difficulties in social interaction. While the link between maternal cell phone use and children's behaviour requires further elucidation, the findings raise important questions about the potential influence of environmental factors on child development.

Overall, while the exact long-term effects of cell phone radiation on children remain subject to ongoing research and debate, the existing evidence stresses the importance of prudent use and moderation, particularly in vulnerable populations such as young children and pregnant women. [17]

All the effects listed and explained here are backed by research and studies. In the next chapter, let's see what AI has in store for us.

## References

[1] Prevalence of excessive screen time and its association with developmental delay in children aged–PubMed (nih.gov)

[2] Prevalence of Screen Time Among Children Aged 2 to 5 Years in Chandigarh, a North Indian Union Territory–PubMed (NIH.gov)

[3] Webster, E. K., Martin, C. K., & Staiano, A. E. (2019). Fundamental motor skills, screen time, and physical activity in preschoolers. Journal of Sport and Health Science, 8(2), 114-121.

[4] https://www.mywellnesshub.in/blog/virtual-autism/

[5] https://www.primescholars.com/proceedings/virtual-autismnew-era-of-autism-spectrum-disorder-outcome-of-indepth-screen-exposure-among-toddlers-aged-14-years-64985.html

[6] https://www.ncbi.nlm.nih.gov/pmc/articles/PMC5849631/

[7] Babies need humans, not screens | UNICEF Parenting

[8] Digital Media and Sleep in Childhood and Adolescence | Pediatrics | American Academy of Pediatrics (aap.org)

[9] Is there a link between screen time and childhood obesity? (activesg.gov.sg)

[10] Investigating Screen Time's Impact on the Attention Span | Discover Magazine

[11] Your Kid Probably Has "Text Neck" – How Phones Cause Back Pain in Children (goodhousekeeping.com)

[12] Repetitive Strain and Distraction Injuries from Screen Use–GetKidsInternetSafe

[13] Associations Between Screen-Based Media Use and Brain White Matter Integrity in Preschool-Aged Children | Neurology | JAMA Pediatrics | JAMA Network

[14] Functional Connectivity of Attention, Visual, and Language Networks During Audio, Illustrated, and Animated Stories in Preschool-Age Children–PubMed (nih.gov)

[15] Internet addiction changes brain similar to cocaine: Study–CBS News

[16] Abnormal White Matter Integrity in Adolescents with Internet Addiction Disorder: A Tract-Based Spatial Statistics Study | PLOS ONE

[17] Children and Cell Phones: Is Phone Radiation Risky for Kids?–Stop Cancer Fund

[18] Babies need humans, not screens | Stop Autism Virtual. https://stopautismvirtual.ro/en/babies-need-humans-not-screens/

[19] Circadian Rhythm–Healthier Tech. https://www.healthier tech.co/glossary/circadian-rhythm/

[20] Is your teen's smartphone literally a pain in the neck? | UCLA Health. https://www.uclahealth.org/news/is-your-teens-smartphone-literally-a-pain-in-the-neck

[21] Is there a link between cell phones and brain cancer?– Neuroscience News. https://neurosciencenews.com/cell-phone-brain-cancer-14922/

[22] Grammarly Generative AI prompts for LogInwards, 2024

[23] Image: https://healthmatters.nyp.org/how-to-prevent-tech-neck/

# Chapter 2

# WHAT AI NOW AND LATER MEANS FOR 0-5-YEAR-OLDS: USING AI WELL, WISELY, AND SAFELY

Artificial intelligence is quickly transforming this world, and its influence is increasing daily. Understanding the impact of AI in the present and future is vital for parents to help their kids develop proper and healthy digital habits and avoid digital addiction. We will discuss the current and potential impacts on children aged 0 to 5 and further extend advice on using these AI tools effectively, appropriately, and responsibly.

## How AI is Impacting Young Children Today?

### a) Artificial Intelligence and Early Childhood Education

AI restructures early childhood education by making learning student-centred for each child. Learning devices, plus apps employing AI, can learn the speed of a child's understanding and provide content at a pace appropriate for their cognitive and early literacy development level. Such tools are truly helpful in identifying and solving problems in learning at an early stage.

Adaptive Learning: AI systems analyse the interaction and progression of the child, changing the difficulty and type of activities so that they are always at the child's learning level.

Speech Recognition: AIs can aid language development by recognising and reacting to a child's speech, promoting verbal expression and proper pronunciation.

## b)  AI in Healthcare

- **Health Monitoring**

AI-powered devices can help monitor the health of young children. For example, the Owlet Smart Sock tracks a baby's heart rate, oxygen levels, and sleep patterns, alerting parents if something seems off. This allows for early detection of potential health issues and provides peace of mind to parents.

- **Virtual Health Assistants**

AI-driven apps like Ada Health can help parents assess their child's symptoms and determine whether they need medical attention. These virtual health assistants use AI to analyse symptoms and provide recommendations based on a vast database of medical knowledge.

## c)  AI in Entertainment

- **Smart Toys**

Smart toys using AI provide many opportunities for enhancing children's learning and development. From international products like Cozmo and Dash and Dot to Indian innovations like Miko and PlayShifu Orboot, these toys offer engaging, personalised, and interactive experiences.

They can recognise faces, play games, and express emotions, making playtime more interactive and enjoyable. These toys can adapt to a child's preferences, providing personalised play experiences. Enlisting a few of them below for your information:

Cozmo by Anki: Cozmo is a small robot that uses AI to recognise faces, express emotions, and play games. It interacts with children through various activities, promoting engagement and learning.

Similarly, Furby Connect is an interactive toy that uses AI to learn words, respond to touch, and engage with children through music and games. It can connect to a mobile app for additional content.

Dash and Dot are programmable robots that teach children basic coding through interactive play. They use AI to perform tasks, respond to voice commands, and interact with their environment.

If I have to give some examples from India, then Miko by Emotix is an AI-powered companion robot designed in India. It engages children in conversations, answers questions, and helps with learning activities. Miko uses AI to understand and respond to the child's emotions.

PlayShifu Orboot is an interactive globe that uses Augmented Reality (AR) to teach children about geography, cultures, and animals. The AI-driven app interacts with the world to provide information and engage children in educational games. It enhances knowledge of geography and cultures and promotes interactive and immersive learning. I have personally seen and tried this one at Hamleys.

Smartykins by Next Education is an AI-enabled educational toy designed to support early learning. They incorporate storytelling, interactive games, and quizzes to engage children in various learning activities.

- **Interactive Storytelling**

AI-driven storytelling apps use AI to adapt stories based on a child's choices, fostering creativity and keeping children engaged. For instance, the app might allow a child to choose a character's path, creating a unique storytelling experience. Here are some examples of such apps for your information:

**International Examples**

Novel Effect uses AI to add sound effects, music, and character voices to books as you read aloud. The app listens to your voice and synchronises sounds and effects to enhance the storytelling experience. It also makes reading more engaging and immersive, encouraging kids to enjoy books and develop a love for reading.

Amazon Rapids offers a library of short stories presented in a chat-style format. The AI recommends stories based on the child's reading level and interests.

HOMER is a personalised learning app that uses AI to tailor stories and learning activities to each child's interests and reading level. The app includes interactive stories and exercises to build literacy skills.

**Indian Examples**

*Karadi Tales* offers a collection of animated and interactive stories based on traditional Indian folklore and contemporary tales. The app uses AI to provide interactive elements and engage children in the story. It introduces children to Indian culture and folklore and enhances their listening and comprehension skills.

Bolo by Google uses AI to help children read aloud and improve their reading skills. The app includes a range of stories and interactive features to assist with pronunciation and comprehension. It supports early literacy in multiple languages, provides personalised reading assistance, and encourages independent reading.

Chimple: Chimple is an AI-powered learning app with interactive stories and activities to teach children foundational literacy and numeracy skills. The app offers personalised learning experiences, engages children with interactive content, and supports holistic development.

## d)  AI in Family Dynamics

- **Virtual Assistants**

Devices like Amazon Echo and Google Home can act as virtual assistants, helping families manage their daily routines. For example, Alexa can remind parents of feeding times, nap schedules, and doctor's appointments. It can also play lullabies or tell bedtime stories, creating a supportive home environment.

- **AI Nannies**

While still in development, AI robots like the 'iPal' are designed to assist with childcare. 'iPal' can engage children in educational activities, monitor their safety, and provide companionship. They are equipped with cameras and sensors to ensure a safe environment and alert parents if something requires their attention.

## The Future Implications of AI for Young Children

### a)  Advances in Customised Education

AI's role in personalised learning will likely increase sophistication and experiences in early childhood education. Future AI systems will be brilliant, sophisticated, and revolutionise early childhood education.

**Improved Adaptation:** AI tools in the future will be able to adjust to what a child is learning now and their interests, emotions, and preferred learning style.

**Global Learning Networks:** AI might connect children from all over the world, generating an understanding of global cultures from a very young age.

**Early Intervention:** Advanced AI systems can identify developmental problems early, helping to devise and effectuate interventions more effectively and promptly.

### b)  Potential Negative Aspects of AI

Though AI provides many opportunities, it also leads to some challenges and risks that parents are supposed to manage with great caution for the well-being of their children.

- **Reduced Creativity and Imagination**

AI-driven toys and apps often provide structured and guided experiences. While these can be educational, they may limit opportunities for children to engage in open-ended play and creative thinking. For example, a child using an AI storytelling app might follow a predefined narrative rather than invent their own stories. This can restrict the development of their imaginative abilities. Another example is a child who spends most of their playtime with an AI-powered robot that suggests games and activities. Over time, the child becomes less interested in playing with non-digital toys or inventing their own games.

- **Decreased Engagement in Traditional Play**

Traditional toys like building blocks, dolls, and art supplies encourage children to use their imagination to create and explore. However, overreliance on AI can reduce the time spent with these toys. So, instead of building a castle with blocks and imagining the adventures of its inhabitants, a child might spend hours interacting with an AI toy that leads the play.

- **Limited Opportunities for Independent Thought**

AI tools often provide quick answers and solutions to problems, which can prevent children from engaging in deep thinking and reasoning. So, a child might ask an AI assistant for homework answers rather than working through the problems themselves, leading to a lack of critical thinking practice.

- **Diminished Analytical Skills**

Critical thinking involves analysing information, questioning assumptions, and evaluating evidence. Overreliance on AI can result in a passive acceptance of information without questioning its validity. So, a child might rely on AI-generated content without learning to critically assess its accuracy or relevance, reducing their ability to think analytically.

- **Effect on Problem-Solving Skills**

  o **Dependency on AI for Solutions**

AI tools are designed to provide solutions and make tasks easier. While convenient, this can hinder the development of problem-solving skills if children rely on AI instead of figuring things out on their own. For example, if a child uses AI to solve a puzzle game, they miss the opportunity to develop the strategies and persistence needed to solve it independently.

  o **Reduced Resilience and Perseverance**

Problem-solving often requires trying multiple approaches and learning from mistakes. More reliance on AI can lead to a lack of perseverance, as children may expect immediate answers and solutions. A child might quickly turn to an AI assistant for help with a challenging task rather than struggling through it, missing out on the learning experience that comes from overcoming difficulties.

- **Data Privacy and Security**

AI tools often collect and store data, leading to privacy and security concerns.

**Data Breaches:** Children's and families' information is unsafe and can be subject to data breaches, which risk the loss of important information and probably lead to security issues like identity theft.

**Unintended Data Use:** Data collected by AI tools might be used for purposes other than what parents consented to, such as targeted advertising.

- **Digital Addiction**

While AI offers valuable tools and resources for children's learning and entertainment, overreliance on these technologies can negatively impact their development of imagination, critical thinking, and problem-solving skills. To mitigate these effects, parents should encourage a balanced approach that includes traditional play, independent learning, and activities that promote creativity and critical thinking. By doing so, children can enjoy the benefits of AI while also developing essential skills for their overall growth and development.

We saw how excessive screen time can affect young children and the present and future implications of AI. Let's see how we can identify whether your child is dependent on technology.

# Chapter 3

# IDENTIFYING SIGNS OF HIGHER DIGITAL DEPENDENCY OR ADDICTION IN YOUR CHILD

This chapter might be a little theoretical, but understanding dependency is quite essential. Let's see what addiction/dependency is, and then it will be easier to understand Digital Dependency.

**"Addiction is a Complex Brain disease expressed in the Form of Compulsive Behaviour despite Harmful Consequences"**

and

**Internet Addiction Disorder is defined as problematic, compulsive use of the internet that results in significant impairment in an individual's function in various life domains over a long period. [6] This is a general disorder where the person is addicted to cyberspace/the internet. There are multiple types of addictions to cyberspace.**

**Types of Internet Addiction (Classified by Young, 1999)**

- Cybersexual addiction (Cybersex and Cyberporn)
- Cyber-relationship addiction (Online relationships)
- Net compulsions (Online shopping, gambling, online trading)

- Information overload (Compulsive web surfing or database searches)
- Computer addiction (Gaming)

In children under five years, we commonly see addiction to gaming and video surfing, including watching reels, shorts, kids' channels, cartoons, etc.

The Diagnostic and Statistical Manual of Mental Disorders, Fifth Edition (DSM-5), provides criteria for diagnosing Internet Gaming Disorder.

**Proposed Criteria Persistent and recurrent use of the Internet to engage in games, often with other players, leading to clinically significant impairment or distress as indicated by five (or more) of the following in 12 months:**

1. **Preoccupation with Internet games:** The individual thinks about previous gaming activity or anticipates playing the next game; Internet gaming becomes the dominant activity in daily life.
2. **Withdrawal symptoms (When Internet gaming is taken away):** These symptoms are typically described as irritability, anxiety, or sadness, but there are no physical signs of pharmacological withdrawal.
3. **Tolerance:** the need to engage more in internet games.
4. **Relapse:** Unsuccessful attempts to control participation in internet games.
5. **Loss of interest in previous hobbies and entertainment** as a result of, and except for, internet games.
6. **Continued excessive use** of Internet games **despite knowledge of psychosocial problems.**
7. **Has deceived** family members, therapists, or others regarding the amount of Internet gaming.

8. **Mood Modification:** Use internet games to escape or relieve a negative mood (e.g., feelings of helplessness, guilt, anxiety).

9. Participation in internet games **has jeopardised or lost a significant relationship, job, or educational or career opportunity.**

Now, based on these criteria and experience in this field, let us see how a child under five years old will present with dependency.

- **Preoccupation:** The child will be preoccupied with thoughts of games, videos, and channels they watch and keep asking for their phone. Whenever you are not around, and your phone is available, the child will start using the phone without your permission.

- **Withdrawal symptoms:** As soon as you tell the child to stop using or take away your phone or gadget from their hands, the child will cry, shout, get angry, might not eat, throw tantrums, blackmail you, or get sad.

- **Tolerance:** Time spent on digital platforms/media keeps increasing. Imagine your child using a gadget for half an hour. Then it will be an hour, two, three, and so on. It is similar to other substance addictions; for example, the way alcoholics drink more and more alcohol to achieve that high. As their body and brain become accustomed to the previous amount of alcohol, they no longer feel the same high and consequently increase their intake.

- **Low impulse control:** They will ask for a few more minutes to play or watch whenever you tell them to keep the screen away, study, or do some work. They cannot keep the screen away and have low impulse control.

- **Unsuccessful attempts to control the usage:** As the child is relatively young, they do not realise this. Usually, parents complain that we tried keeping him away from screens, but we were unsuccessful.

- **Loss of interest:** Loss of interest in playing with his friends, outdoor play, art activities, or activities the child loved before.

- **Hiding and lying:** The child hides and lies about their screen usage. They may use gadgets in the absence of parents or caretakers.

- **Mood modification:** If the child is upset, sad, angry, or afraid, their mood changes as soon as the screen is given. The child will manipulate their parents into giving them screens by crying or being upset. They know that if they are upset or cry, their parents or caretaker will provide them with the screen.

- **Decreased interaction:** The child stops interacting with family members and friends, which affects their studies as they are no longer interested in them.

**In addition, we must also consider the effects on physical health and development mentioned in the previous chapter.**

If you see any signs or symptoms, be alert and take the required steps. At the end of the book, a detailed Early Childhood Device Usage Assessment (EC-DUA) for 2-to 5-year-old children is available for you to assess your child's device usage.

# Chapter 4

# IDEAL SCREEN TIME LIMITS

The Indian Psychiatric Society has given the following recommendations for screen use for children up to five years of age.

- Parents should altogether **avoid screens for children under two years of age.**
- For children **aged two to five years**, introducing digital media content is not necessarily an entitlement or necessity. If introduced, it is always preferred to be under parental or adult guidance and monitoring.
- For children between two and five years of age, **viewing should be introduced for specific purposes, such as educational games or teaching aids for a limited period (not longer than 30 minutes per session, and not more than two sessions per day, under supervision—a shared media use) rather than for entertainment. Adult interaction with the child during media use is crucial. For small children, knowledge gained through the media is not easily transferred to the real-life three-dimensional world.**
- Avoid fast-paced programmes and apps with lots of distracting content, as this can make concentration difficult later. Also, avoid any violent content.

# Chapter 5

# WALK THE TALK

**Your Role as Parents in Inculcating Screen Discipline**

Observing people has become a favourite pastime of mine. Wherever I go, I observe parents and their interactions, particularly regarding screen use and parenting.

A concerning trend I have noticed is the prevalence of infants and toddlers watching YouTube videos while eating. Parents and grandparents often do this to ensure their child eats without fuss. They justify it by saying they only show them age-appropriate content, like rhymes. Some even believe it helps their child eat more, leading to weight gain, which they perceive as a positive outcome. It is alarming to witness the pride some parents take when their very young children can navigate YouTube and select their favourite videos.

In many households, both parents work, leaving children under the care of grandparents or other caregivers. Unfortunately, many grandparents lack the energy and patience to engage children actively, resorting to screens as distractions. With parents away, they feel they have no authority to intervene in their child's screen time, leading to a lack of control over their digital habits.

While visiting a nearby garden, I often see parents engrossed in their mobile phones while their children play. Despite their children's attempts to seek attention and share their achievements, parents glance up briefly before returning to their screens. Instead of cherishing these moments of free play, parents prioritise their devices or phone calls.

Parents often come home after a long workday to bury themselves in their phones or TV screens. They justify this behaviour as their only opportunity to catch up on messages and social media. However, this precious time should be reserved for bonding with family and spending quality time with their children. Unfortunately, screen time often hijacks these family moments.

Some parents admit to watching TV only during mealtime, assuming it is harmless. However, when questioned about their child's screen time, they fail to recognise the inconsistency in their behaviour. They overlook the importance of setting a positive example for their children.

I have witnessed countless parents scolding their children for excessive screen time while glued to their screens. Children learn by observing their parents' actions, not just their words. If parents want to see changes in their children's behaviour, they must reflect on their habits and make necessary adjustments. They will only see meaningful results in their children's screen time habits.

**Parental Behaviours That Contribute to Increased Screen Time in Children Under Five**

### 1) Giving screens during mealtime

This has become a new trend among most parents and grandparents. When you show videos to the child while feeding, the child eats peacefully and effortlessly.

Everyone is happy!

Parents and grandparents are happy that mealtime is shortened!

The child is happy to watch the videos!

Most caretakers do not know that screen time during mealtime will distract children from feeling physiological satiety. Children will not realise when to stop, leading to mindless eating and overeating habits. This is one of the significant factors for childhood obesity. By giving them screens at mealtime, we are also preparing them for binge eating in the future. Children will not enjoy the food; they will enjoy screens while having food. When we ask these children what they ate at the last meal, they are clueless.

## 2)  Using gadgets as pacifiers when they are bored or upset

Children tend to get bored quickly, and it takes a few seconds for them to get upset and cry!

Many parents hand over their phones when their child starts crying or irritating them, saying, "Mumma, I am getting bored", or "Dad, I am getting bored."

One thing I have noticed, and many parents have told me, is that our child is responsible for not getting bored. The child should be constantly happy, busy, or entertained. You are a parent, not a joker. Parents think they are failing if their child gets bored, but they do not know that boredom is an opportunity for their child to be creative. Boredom brings out a lot of creativity in the child. When children get bored, they wear a thinking cap and find new ways to be busy or entertained. If, as parents, you give them smartphones or iPads whenever they are bored, they will never learn to overcome their boredom through creativity. They will stop using their brains. You will make them slaves to technology!

Similarly, if the child is angry or upset and crying, giving the child a phone to make him stop crying will do more harm to your child than you think. In the long-term, the child will learn to use digital platforms to soothe his negative emotions rather than come to you and talk openly about them. Various digital platforms will always be there for him, and he can forget his worries and fears. I have seen the same parents complaining about their children later in life, saying their children do not communicate with them. Children are busy with their gadgets, and parents do not know what is happening in their lives. Obviously! You will not know! You have not taught him the same!

When your child cries, it is more important to know and validate his feelings. Knowing why he is upset, communicating with him, and addressing his emotions will teach him how to be aware of his own emotions and manage them rather than escaping into the world of technology. This will also teach him to be mindful of others' emotions and manage them when upset.

## 3) Using gadgets in front of your child even when you are not working

Whenever I tell parents who come for their child's counselling for screen time reduction, I ask them to stop using gadgets in front of their child when free and not doing any work. There is a reason behind this. If you want to teach screen discipline to your child, you also have to follow some screen discipline. When your child is around, and you are free, utilise your time either playing with him or doing any recreational activity like reading, art, yoga, exercise, etc. When the child sees you utilising your free time like this, it tells his brain that whenever we are free, we should utilise our time like this rather than using gadgets. Children do not learn from what you say, they learn from what you see. And if there is a contradiction in your actions and what you say, they will follow what you do, not what you say.

Many parents tell me, "But Madam, we check our phones and find time to check messages only when we come home from work. If we do not even check at that time, then when?"

You must be aware of your hour-by-hour timetable from when you wake up. You will find at least one hour during the day when your child is not around, and you can check your messages, scroll through your social media profile, or do whatever you want. If, as an adult, you cannot follow and stick to the timetable, how reasonable is it to expect from your kids?

## 4) Phubbing

Looking at a screen and not paying attention while your child tries to communicate with you greatly impacts children. Imagine you are telling your boss something important, but your boss is busy on their phone and not paying enough attention to you. How would you feel?

When kids try to communicate with you, everything is quite important to them (it might not be for you). If you listen to them without paying enough attention or looking at your gadget, it will not go down well with your kids. Firstly, kids will feel that what they want to communicate is unimportant. Secondly, they will learn to speak in the same manner. Years later, parents complain that their child is not listening to them and is constantly on his phone.

**Listening and communicating with your child**

- Stop phubbing, start listening!
- If you are busy and your child comes to talk, tell them you are busy and will be free soon.
- Let him know that if you talk now, it will not be with full attention, and you will not like that because it might be something important.
- Give him a specific time, and then have an active conversation.
- Keep your gadget aside and listen to anyone who tries to converse with you.
- Maintain eye contact throughout the conversation.
- Pay 100% attention to what they say.
- Do not interrupt.
- After they have stopped speaking, ask questions wherever necessary. This will signal to the other person that you are listening attentively.

I have seen that this not only improves the bond with kids but also enhances almost all relationships.

Try it!

## 5) Giving a gadget to your child because you want to have some peaceful time for yourself

As the mother of a naughty 2-year-old boy, I completely understand how difficult it is to find some peaceful time for yourself! But giving any gadget to your kid for your quiet time will sow the seeds of digital addiction. As I have mentioned before, know your day. Plan your 'Me' time when your kid is not around or when someone else can take responsibility for your kid and enjoy your time with yourself. It is necessary for your mental health but avoid giving a gadget to your kid.

## 6) Not saying NO if they ask for your phone or any gadget from you

Kids are so smart! They know when to ask for your phone or iPad. I have seen kids asking for gadgets when parents talk with someone, when guests are at home, if they are getting bored at a family function, when parents are busy at work or on a work call, etc. Kids know and have learned from their experiences that whenever my parents are in public or busy, they will not say no if I ask. You do not want your child to cry in public, tarnishing your image as a parent. You do not want to be disturbed while working or talking, so even when you know your actions are incorrect, you still do that. Nothing is wrong with it, but your kid will start manipulating you, looking at your weaknesses.

Whatever happens, your answer should be a 'NO' as a parent of a child under five years old. You are not supposed to give the gadget to your child. You are supposed to co-watch! Screen use guidelines—remember?

## 7) Praising them regarding their screen use in front of other people

"My 2-year-old son can go on YouTube and watch his favorites rhyme by himself!"

"My 4-year-old daughter can go to the Play Store and download games she wants to play alone!"

So many parents feel a sense of pride when discussing screen use of their children. I feel pity! They do not know what they are sowing. We all know that when children are praised for a specific behavior, they tend to engage in that behavior more. If you praise them regarding their screen use in front of others, this signals that this is an accepted behavior, and I am supposed to do this more so that I get appreciated a little more. They will explore more and show that to you. This cycle will continue every time with feedback that it is okay to use screens.

As the screen use guidelines mention, children under five should not be given gadgets to use independently, i.e. not under parental guidance. This brings us to our next point.

## 8) Giving them gadgets without monitoring or co-watching

Why a guideline like this? Many parents ask me when they come for counselling.

The idea is simple. There will be no control over what the children are using gadgets for. Usually, children use their parents' phones, laptops, or tablets. Parents, being adults, might have searched or surfed anything that an adult is supposed to read or watch. We all know that based on our search histories, we start getting ads even when using another app. As Google accounts are linked to all devices now, ads appear on your phone apps even if you have searched for something on your laptop. Just imagine if one of the parents has watched porn recently or shopped for lingerie; related ads might pop-up when the child is using a phone for anything. We have seen cases where children have had early exposure to these things because they accidentally clicked on a pop-up while using their parents' phone to play a game, and parents had no idea about it!

Hence, co-watching on a separate device is always advisable. Also, if giving the child a phone or any other gadget is unavoidable, using parental control apps is mandatory to monitor their usage.

**Now, let's discuss how you can sow the seeds of screen discipline for your child until the age of five.**

As we already read in the Ideal Screen time Recommendations by the Indian Psychiatric Society,

**For children between 2 and 5 years of age, introducing digital media content is not necessarily an entitlement or necessity.**

**But,**

**If introduced, it is always preferred to be under parental or adult guidance and monitoring.**

So, if you want to introduce screens to your child, the following pointers will help you sow the seeds of screen discipline.

## 1) Set a routine for your child and a fixed time for co-watching the screen

If you have set a routine for your child for brushing teeth, meals, school time, nap time, playtime, reading time, garden time, etc., it becomes easier to set a fixed time for co-watching screens with your child. The child knows they have to follow a schedule and will not be given a screen beyond that time. Once the child is used to this routine, they will not cry if you stop showing them the screen because they know their half an hour of screen time is over now. But, if you set a routine just for screen time and no other things, it might be difficult for the child to follow the screening timetable. Screen time should be made like a daily habit of fixed duration at a fixed time rather than giving any time of the day for an undecided duration. Now, if your child goes to a school where they teach on screen and the child learns on screens too, you can decide for your child if you want to introduce extra screen time at this age or not. If yes, setting up a fixed time and duration is advisable.

## 2) Plan your child's screen time

As parents, you can plan your child's screen time. You can prepare for a week, just like some couples plan their meals. Firstly, decide the purpose for you to co-watch with your child. The purpose can vary each week. Typical purposes of co-watching can include teaching, playing educational games and puzzles, introducing music, rhymes, jingles, co-watching a sport, etc. You can decide the purpose of the week's plan in advance for your child and make a timetable for the week. You can make it exciting and display it on a board or your fridge where the child can see it.

How does this help? It builds excitement in the child. The child will wait for the programme and enjoy watching it with you. Again, when you have made a timetable, it tells the kid that they have to follow this timetable, and the child will learn to follow it. By planning, you can be clear about what you want to introduce to your child, and your content will be focused and have a definite purpose.

## 3)  Discuss while co-watching

When introducing media with a purpose, pause and discuss every time there is something to learn from it. Ask your children what they observed. How did they feel? What did they learn? Listen to them without any judgements or interruptions, and once they are done, explain your point of view. If you have introduced educational games, take feedback after the game and give it to your children.

How does this help? It helps create a bond and a strong base for communication. It signals to them that I can tell and talk freely to this person. My parents are open to listening to what I have to say. When you give them your feedback without judging what they learn, they learn about different perspectives. They will know that two people can view the same thing differently. This learning goes a long way.

## 4)  Screen-free family fun time

Just like you set a routine for everything else, set a time for "Screen-free family fun time". Now, depending on your schedule on weekdays and weekends, you can have it daily, on alternate days, or at weekends. Have at least a few hours a week where the whole family spends time without gadgets. You can talk, discuss a topic, paint, sing, dance, walk, have a picnic, trek, play board games, do puzzles, meditate, do yoga, or whatever you want for that fixed interval of time on that day.

How does this help? When the whole family comes together and gets involved in a fun activity, this becomes bonding time for the entire family. The child will remember this, becoming a core memory of his life. Also, when the family is having screen-free fun, the child will learn ways to communicate effectively without screens. If you do not teach children to have fun without screens, they will think that the only way to have fun is to play games on the phone or video games or watch videos, reels, and shorts mindlessly. Children tend to get bored quite quickly, and the most accessible pacifier available then is a screen. They do not think beyond that. So, if you expose them to screen-free fun activities, they will have many options to break their boredom. Why is it important? Because boredom is the most common trigger for children to use screens. If they have learned to cope with their boredom, they will not only take the aid of screens.

## 5)  Utilising Weekends

In working parents' lives, weekends are essential to bond with your children and take them out. Spending maximum time with your children on weekends is more than necessary. You can spare at least one day out of the 2 weekend days for your children. On the other day, you can plan or do your planning for the next week if you have to. Take them out for a picnic, outing, long drive, trekking, gardens, nature park, cycling, take them for a beautiful play, take them to play areas, museums, zoo, etc. If there is a good movie for children coming up, plan that too and, as mentioned before, discuss post-movie so that you can enhance the experience for the child.

## 6)  Introduce your child to different emotions and emotional fingerprints

What is the role of introducing emotions in the screen discipline or balance? Emotional awareness and management skills are critical when preparing your child for the future. While treating tweens and teenagers, we have seen many cases where the most typical reasons for them to go to screens are boredom, feeling low, anxious, angry, fear of missing out (FOMO), loneliness, and feeling disconnected. Digital media and platforms become their friends in need when running away from these emotions, so they become their friends indeed. Most kids do not know what they feel, why they go online, or what they think online. They escape from their negative emotions or difficult life situations into cyberspace. Most of them are very poor at emotional intelligence skills. They are unaware of their feelings and do not know how to manage them. Children who are taught emotional intelligence skills from a very young age grow up with good emotional awareness and management skills. Introducing emotional vocabulary to your toddler or preschooler is the first step to raising an emotionally intelligent child. What should you do? Introduce them to various basic emotions through pictures, emojis, and stories. Whenever they have any feelings, say them out loud. For example, if your child is angry and crying, say, "It seems you are angry." They will learn to label their emotions, which is the first step in emotional awareness. We are making them emotionally literate.

Now, let's see what feeling fingerprints are. Feeling fingerprints are physical signs or stamps of different emotions. For example, if we feel angry, our body feels hot, our heartbeat increases, our face turns red (flushed), and the body might tremble. So, these physical signs are feeling fingerprints for the emotion 'Anger'. Just like that, different emotions will generate different signs in the body. Introducing kids to feeling fingerprints also helps identify their feelings and labelling. Once you have introduced them to various emotions, ask them what they think whenever they feel something. If they identify correctly, praise them; if they do not, correct them. Keep on doing this exercise with fun. You can also find games and stories to introduce this concept. Make it fun-filled rather than considering it as a task.

## 7)  Delayed gratification

Delayed gratification is an essential concept not only concerning parenting but also as an emotional intelligence skill. This particular skill can determine many future outcomes for your child. The definition of delayed gratification is the ability to postpone an impulse for an immediate reward or pleasure to achieve a more significant purpose at a later time. Simplifying for you, it is the ability to choose larger goals over immediate gratification or pleasure.

In the Stanford Marshmallow experiment, psychologist Walter Mischel gave children a choice. They were given a treat in the form of marshmallows. They could enjoy one marshmallow now or wait a few more minutes to get two. When the experimenter left the room, many kids ate the marshmallows immediately. Still, some of the kids were able to wait for the reward of getting two delicious marshmallows later on.

The kids were then followed through and analysed until they grew up. Mischel discovered that the kids who could delay gratification had several advantages later on over those who could not. The children who had delayed their urge for the marshmallows performed better academically and had fewer behavioural problems than those with no impulse control.

Walter Mischel states, "The good news is that this cognitive and emotional skill set is eminently teachable, particularly early in life. It is great in preschool and within the first few years of life. It is great in adolescence too. And it continues to be a skill set that can be developed even when we are quite mature adults". [1]

Now, you must be wondering how this can help build healthy screen time habits in the child. As mentioned, impulse control is one of the most significant skills regarding healthy screen habits. Teaching impulse control techniques and delaying pleasures will help discipline the child regarding screen time and in the future. If the child develops these skills early, they can delay the impulse to use screens and seek pleasure. They understand the importance of higher goals in life.

## Empowering Your Child to Choose Patience Over Instant Gratification

### Gratification-Delaying Child

- **Self-Control:** More restrained and patient; they realise that waiting usually brings better rewards.
- **Long-term Goals:** The child understands that often, one must set aside short-term pleasures for the more significant long-term advantages of an action.
- **Solving Problems:** They generally approach problems calmly and are willing to continue working on challenging tasks rather than finding them frustrating and beyond their competence.
- **Emotional Regulation:** Generally, they manage their emotions better and tolerate frustration and disappointment.
- **Higher Academic and Social Success:** Children who can delay gratification usually show higher academic performance later in life and fare better in social settings due to their resilience to setbacks.

## Child Who Wants Everything Now

- **Impulsivity:** This child will act impulsively, want things now, and not consider what can happen because of their actions.
- **Difficulty Managing Emotions:** They could have frustration issues, get easily upset when their way does not happen, and find waiting very difficult to cope with.
- **Focus on Immediate Pleasures:** They do not think of the future benefits but rather want immediate pleasures, which create difficulty in situations like overeating, excessive screen time, or unfinished tasks.
- **Goal Attainment Issues:** Not being able to delay gratification, this child will quickly give up when a hindrance comes because he wants the same thing immediately.
- **Impact on Relationships and Academics:** Instant gratification might also impact relationships or academics through impatient outbursts, conflict, or an inability to focus.

## Yes, You Can Teach Even a Small Child the Value of Delayed Gratification!

- **Children learn from you**

As mentioned, they will learn the same if you walk the talk. You can tell your child, "I feel like watching this movie on the OTT platform, but my work is my priority. So, I will watch it once my work is over." And when you do that, tell your child, "See! Because I finished my work, I watched the movie peacefully." Or "I could have watched a movie anytime, but work was urgent, so obviously, it made sense to do my work first. Now I can enjoy my movie".

Similarly, show them that you delay different pleasures for more essential things like household chores, reading, spending time with family, etc. Seeing you do the same, they will also learn to prioritise their work over pleasure.

When they demand something, do not give that thing right away.

My parents used to do this with us (my brother and me). If I asked for a dress, my mom would say, "I cannot give it to you right now, but we will buy it on Diwali". She would buy me that dress on Diwali, but I had to wait. I eagerly waited for Diwali, and I used to feel happy when I got the dress. My parents would always keep their word.

Similarly, we had to wait to eat out, buy clothes, and buy toys. Sometimes, if finances were not favourable, they would tell us that this would not be possible because of financial constraints, but instead, we could do something else. I remember us being okay with this compromise. We would get so angry as children that we had to wait for everything. Still, when I first learned about delayed gratification and its positive effects later in life, I remembered my childhood and was thankful to my parents. This skill has helped me a lot throughout my life in various ways.

- **Delay the craving/impulse**

When the child feels too impulsive and craves something, teach them how to distract their mind. The technique is called **the 4D method.**

  o **Delay the craving**–Cravings rise and fall like waves. Delaying the craving for 20 minutes can dissipate the cravings on their own.

- o **Distract**–Delay the craving by making them do something else, like counting backwards, jumping, drawing, dancing, Om chanting, etc. Strategise what works for your child. Teach them a grounding technique and ask them to name five things they can see, five sounds they hear, anything they can smell or touch, and how it feels. Use special senses to ground them and distract them.
- o **Deep breathing**–Teach them deep breathing and pranayama when they get the impulse.
- o **Drink water**–Let them drink water slowly and mindfully

- **Ask them questions and let them choose**

Whenever they demand a phone or a device, ask them why they want it. What are they going to do? Is there anything else important right now, and can this be delayed? Give them options for activities instead of spending their time on screens. Let them choose from the options you gave them. Once they have done that activity, reflect with them. What did they learn? Did they enjoy it? What part of the activity did they enjoy? How did they feel while doing that activity, and always have closure of that activity?

- **Reward self-control**

Whenever they practise self-control and are successful, reward them in various ways. You can make reward cards and write different rewards on them. Whenever they are successful, let them choose one reward card and give that reward to them. Parents and children can mutually decide on rewards.

- **Communicating openly**

It is essential to foster an environment that encourages your child to speak openly about anything. Why is it important? As parents, you must be aware of the risks posed by technology. If your child is experiencing anything negative while using their digital device, they need to know they can converse with you about the situation. With the rise of social media and gaming, instances of cyberbullying are becoming quite common. This is why you must remind your child from a very young age that they can raise any issue they feel uncomfortable with. [2]

## 8) Communicating about problematic and healthier usage of technology

The tech addiction treatment field has identified healthier screen usage versus more problematic screen exposure. Screen exposure that is purely titillating or of the adrenaline rush variety (addictive and hyper-stimulating) is considered Digital Candy.

(Ref: 'Glow Kids' by Nicholas Kardaras, Ph.D.)

| Problematic screen exposure (Digital Candy) | Healthier screen usage (Digital vegetables) |
|---|---|
| Video games | E-mailing |
| Mindless YouTube Surfing | Educational YouTube videos |
| Internet Porn Watching | Skyping a friend |
| Hyper-texting | Creating Music or Following a Sports Team |
| Hyper-Social Media | |
| Internet surfing to research a topic | |

When you are using your phone or laptop in front of your child while working, explain to them why you are using it and the benefits of technology concerning work, academics, and others. Talking about the healthy use of technology and its benefits is equally important. The child will understand that it is not all bad and that they must use technology responsibly, carefully, and appropriately. Similarly, talking about the problematic use of technology and its consequences will make them more responsible and help them make better choices in using technology. Discussing the pros and cons of technology from such a young age decreases the chances of developing addiction at a later age manifold.

## 9) Storytelling

Introducing screen discipline through stories is the best way to communicate this to your child. Children love stories, and just as you teach morning routine, bedtime routine, and potty training through books, you can introduce the concept of screen time routine to your child through books. You can also teach them what they will miss out on if their screen time is excessive. You can be creative and make your own stories, too.

## 10) Screen Time Reward Schedule

Lastly, creating a screen time reward schedule can help manage screen use while encouraging positive behaviour and setting healthy boundaries. Here is a guide to help you build one:

### 1. Set Clear Daily Limits

Establish a baseline of acceptable screen time per day (e.g., 1-2 hours) based on your child's age, daily routine, and needs.

## 2. Define Earning Criteria

Children can 'earn' screen time by completing tasks, chores, or positive behaviours. This reinforces that screen time is a privilege earned through good actions.

Basic daily tasks (non-negotiable): Finish homework, clean up toys, brush teeth, etc.

Extra rewards: Completing additional chores, showing kindness, practising hobbies (reading, playing outside).

Example:

Finish homework on time = ten extra minutes of screen time.

Complete additional chores (e.g., folding laundry) = 5 extra minutes.

## 3. Screen Time 'Bank' or Token System

Implement a reward system where children accumulate screen time tokens, points, or a time 'bank'. The child earns minutes of screen time for each task completed, which they can redeem later.

5 points = 1 minute of screen time.

50 points = 10 minutes of screen time.

## 4. Structured Time Slots

Set specific time frames when earned screen time can be used. For example:

Weekdays: Screen time can be between 6-8 pm.

Weekends: Screen time can be between 9-11 am or 4-6 pm.

This prevents screen time from interfering with more important activities (like schoolwork or family time).

## 5. Daily/Weekly Reset

Unused screen time does not roll over to the next day or week to ensure a healthy balance and avoid excessive screen time build-up.

## 6. Encourage Breaks

Incorporate short breaks to rest your eyes and move around during longer screen sessions. For instance:

Every 15 minutes of screen time = 10 minutes of physical activity or a break

## 7. Fun Visual Tracker

Create a fun chart or digital tracker where children can track their progress in earning screen time. You can make this visual by adding stickers, stars, or points.

| Task / Behaviour | Screen Time Earned |
| --- | --- |
| Homework completion | 10 minutes |
| Extra reading (15 minutes) | 5 minutes |
| Helping with dinner | 5 minutes |
| Kind behaviour towards a sibling | 5 minutes |
| Completing daily chores | 5 minutes |
| Bedtime on time | 10 minutes |

By rewarding screen time for good behaviour and accomplishments, children will be more motivated to manage their time and responsibilities effectively.

# References

[1] Mischel W, Shoda Y, Rodriguez MI. Delay of gratification in children. Science. 1989;244(4907):933-938. doi: 10.1126/science.2658056

[2] Parenting In The Digital Age: Technology Tips | Findmykids. https://findmykids.org/blog/en/parenting-in-the-digital-age

[3] Grammarly Generative AI prompts for LogInwards, 2024

# Chapter 6

# PARENTING STYLES AND INTERNET ADDICTION

In a recent study conducted in February 2021, researchers examined the relationship between perceived parenting styles and internet addiction among university students. The study found that different parenting styles resulted in varying levels of internet addiction. Specifically, the authoritarian parenting style emerged as the most potent risk factor for internet addiction, followed by the permissive parenting style. Conversely, authoritative parenting was associated with a lower level of internet addiction among university students.

Similarly, a study conducted in January 2018 in Kuala Lumpur, Malaysia, explored the impact of parenting styles and parental attachment on overcoming internet addiction in children. The findings revealed that children who experienced explicit parental control, a healthy home environment, and secure attachments with their parents reported less internet risk behaviour. Additionally, parental support was identified as a crucial factor in promoting safer internet usage and aiding in the prevention and overcoming of internet addiction. However, the study also highlighted adverse outcomes associated with parenting styles lacking warmth and involvement, such as increased levels of problem behaviour.

These studies underscore the significant influence of parenting styles on children's internet risk behaviour and the importance of parental support in addressing internet addiction. Now, let's delve into the different types of parenting styles.

Parenting styles refer to the approaches or methodologies adopted by parents in raising their children. Diana Baumrind, a renowned clinical and developmental psychologist, identified the following parenting styles: authoritative, authoritarian, and permissive/indulgent. Later, Maccoby and Martin introduced the uninvolved/neglectful style. Understanding these parenting styles is crucial in comprehending their impact on children's development and behaviour, including their relationship with technology and internet usage. [1][2][3]

## Types of Parenting Styles

Parenting styles have two main components: Parental support, responsiveness, involvement, warmth, and demandingness, as well as control and strictness.

### 1)  Authoritative Parenting Style

Authoritative parents, or 'Democratic parents', balance high demands and warmth. They encourage open communication and engage in rational discussions with their children. These parents listen to their child's perspective while providing guidance and setting clear rules and reasonable expectations. Additionally, authoritative parents are empathetic, emotionally intelligent, and responsive to their child's needs. They positively enforce discipline, considering the child's interests while explaining their behaviour's consequences.

Children raised by authoritative parents tend to be happy, emotionally intelligent, independent, academically successful, and possess strong social skills, with fewer mental health issues or addictions.

## 2) Authoritarian Parenting Style

Authoritarian parents exhibit high demands but low warmth in their parenting approach. Often called 'Dictators' or 'Disciplinarians', these parents enforce strict rules and expect obedience without question. They give harsh punishments for mistakes and provide minimal explanation. Authoritarian parents have high expectations, are critical, and impose rigid rules without flexibility. While they may hover over their children to prevent mistakes, little warmth or emotional support is shown. Children raised by authoritarian parents are more likely to experience mental health issues, have lower self-esteem, struggle with independence, possess poor emotional intelligence, exhibit poor academic performance, and have limited social skills, with a higher susceptibility to addictions.

## 3) Permissive/Indulgent Parenting Style

Permissive parents demonstrate low demands but high warmth in their parenting style. They adopt a non-punitive, accepting, and affirmative approach towards their children's behaviour, offering abundant freedom without restrictions. Children are often granted complete autonomy, with little to no expectations for responsibility or orderly behaviour. Permissive parents prioritise warmth and love, sometimes using material rewards to influence their children's behaviour. They may act more like friends than authoritative figures.

However, children of permissive parents tend to be less happy, lack respect for authority, struggle with self-control, exhibit rule-breaking behaviour, face challenges in social settings, experience poor mental health, and struggle with emotional regulation, often displaying stubbornness and an insistence on having their way.

## 4) Neglectful/Uninvolved Parenting Style

Neglectful or uninvolved parents demonstrate low demands and low warmth in their parenting approach. They exhibit minimal involvement in their children's lives, showing little interest, affection, or emotional support. These parents often let their children raise themselves, providing little guidance or structure. They spend little time with their children and have minimal expectations. Children of neglectful parents typically experience poor mental health, low self-esteem, anxiety, stress, difficulty coping with emotions, higher susceptibility to addictions, and an increased likelihood of engaging in criminal behaviour as adolescents. Additionally, they often struggle academically due to the lack of parental involvement and support. [4][5]

**Internet-related Behaviour of These Four Parenting Styles**

These four parenting styles manifest differently in internet-related behaviour, shaping children's digital habits and tendencies.

1.  **Authoritative Parenting:** In a cyber-context, authoritative parents establish clear rules and screen time limits for their children. They provide essential knowledge on digital literacy, online threats, and the consequences of excessive screen time. These parents maintain open

communication with their children, staying informed about the latest technology and its pros and cons. While fostering understanding and care, they exercise control where necessary, setting balanced boundaries in the digital age.

2. **Authoritarian Parenting:** Authoritarian parents impose strict rules and demand obedience without providing adequate explanations or understanding. Punishment is used for non-compliance, and communication tends to be one-sided, favouring the parent's directives. Due to the lack of explanation and dialogue, this approach can lead to unhealthy internet behaviour and potential addiction.

3. **Permissive/Indulgent Parenting:** Permissive parents prioritise their children's needs and maintain open communication and affection but fail to establish firm rules or boundaries. Children often dictate terms, with parents readily granting their requests for gadgets, gaming, and unrestricted internet access. This overly permissive approach, driven by the child's desires, can contribute to unhealthy internet habits and addiction.

4. **Neglectful/Uninvolved Parenting:** Neglectful parents exhibit minimal involvement and fail to provide their children with love, communication, or guidance. They set no rules or limits regarding internet usage, demonstrating a lack of concern or care for their child's well-being. Children raised in such environments are particularly vulnerable to the adverse effects of unrestricted internet access and lack of parental oversight.

In summary, parenting style significantly influences children's internet behaviour and the risk of internet addiction. Understanding these dynamics is crucial for parents seeking to navigate the complexities of raising children in the digital age. The next chapter will delve into practical challenges parents encounter when attempting to instil screen discipline in their children.

## References

[1] (PDF) Perceived Parenting Styles and Internet Addiction among University Students (researchgate.net)

[2] (PDF) A study on Parenting Styles and Parental Attachment in Overcoming Internet Addiction among Children (researchgate.net)

[3] Baumrind's Parenting Styles is an adaptation of Child, Family, and Community (Chapter 6: A Closer Look at Parenting) by Laff & Ruiz (2019), licensed CC BY 4.0, and Social and Personality Development in Childhood by Ross Thompson, licensed CC BY NC SA.

[4] Diana Baumrind Parenting Styles | GoStudent | GoStudent

[5] EFFECTS OF AUTHORITATIVE PARENTAL CONTROL ON CHILD BEHAVIOUR. (wabash.edu)

[6] Level of Internet Addiction among School-going Adolescents. https://paper.researchbib.com/view/paper/287725

[7] Grammarly Generative AI Prompts for LogInwards, 2024

# Chapter 7

# PRACTICAL PROBLEMS FACED BY WORKING PARENTS AND THEIR POSSIBLE SOLUTIONS

In today's fast-paced world, working parents face unique challenges in managing their children's screen time while juggling their professional responsibilities. Whether in a nuclear family, semi-nuclear family, or joint family setup, the demands of work often intersect with the need to ensure a healthy balance of screen time for children. Here, we explore some common practical problems faced by working parents in different family setups and offer possible solutions to address them:

## 1) Nuclear Family

In a nuclear family setup consisting solely of parents and the child, working parents often face the challenge of ensuring their child's well-being and screen time management while they are away for work. Here are two common scenarios and practical solutions:

### Daycare Option

Selecting one that aligns with your preferences and values is crucial when opting for daycare. Consider the following factors:

- Ensure the daycare facility has CCTV access for real-time monitoring.
- Confirm that the daycare environment does not include screens or electronic gadgets, especially in smaller home-based setups.
- Assess the availability of engaging activities to keep your child entertained and stimulated.
- Research and gather feedback from other parents about their experiences with the chosen daycare.
- Maintain communication with fellow parents to share information about ideal screen time limits and the risks of excessive screen time. This collective awareness can encourage consistency in parenting approaches and foster a supportive environment for all daycare children.

**Caregiver at Home**

If you opt to hire a caregiver to look after your child at home while you work, consider the following precautions:

- Restrict the areas of the house accessible to the caregiver by locking bedrooms and other off-limits areas.
- Create a dedicated living room or kitchen space for your child›s essentials to ensure controlled access.
- Install CCTV cameras in critical areas of the house to monitor the caregiver›s interactions with your child.
- Secure any electronic devices, such as TVs, and establish clear guidelines regarding screen time limits and usage.
- Provide the caregiver with a structured timetable for your child›s activities, including designated TV time for older children.
- Communicate expectations regarding phone usage, allowing only essential calls in the child›s presence.

By implementing these measures and maintaining open communication with caregivers, parents can ensure a safe and conducive environment for their child's development and screen time management, even in their absence. Upon returning home, parents can plan and adjust their child's routine according to their preferences and schedule.

## 2) Semi-nuclear Family setup includes parents, in-laws, and the child

In a semi-nuclear family where both parents work, childcare often involves a combination of grandparents and a caregiver. Here is how to navigate this scenario effectively:

### Childcare by Grandparents

When grandparents take care of the child in the parent's absence, there are inherent challenges due to differences in energy levels and patience. These challenges can impact discipline, including managing screen time. Common consequences include:

- Grandparents may use screens to entertain or soothe the child, especially when tired or overwhelmed.
- They may need to fully understand the consequences of excessive screen time and its impact on the child›s development.
- Parents may hesitate to intervene or enforce rules, knowing that the grandparents provide care.
- Even if parents communicate their concerns, implementing changes in screen time management may be challenging when parents are away.

## Minimising Damage

- To mitigate these challenges and minimise the risk of unhealthy screen behaviour, consider the following steps:
- Approach the situation with humility and gratitude towards the grandparents, fostering open communication.
- Have a detailed conversation with the grandparents about the effects of excessive screen time, internet addiction, and the importance of setting boundaries.
- Seek their input on practical difficulties they face and collaborate on finding solutions to implement screen time alternatives.
- Create a structured timetable for childcare activities, including designated screen-free periods, to provide consistent guidance.
- Be patient and understanding, acknowledging that change may take time and effort.
- Regularly check in with the grandparents to assess progress and address any difficulties or concerns.
- Consider hiring a caretaker to share the workload and provide additional support if feasible.
- Upon returning home, engage with your child directly, focusing on skill-building activities and quality time together.
- Lead by example by adhering to the exact timetable and rules, consistently reinforcing positive behaviour.

The ideal setup involves a caretaker working alongside grandparents, ensuring the child receives adequate care, supervision, and attention while adhering to established guidelines.

## 3) Joint family setup

There are unique challenges in managing screen time for children in a joint family setup, which can comprise more than 5-6 people with varying relationships. While there are numerous benefits to raising a child in a joint family, such as learning to interact with many individuals and developing social skills, there are also specific obstacles to implementing screen discipline:

- Due to many family members, restricting screen usage in front of the child may prove difficult.
- Some people may have differing views or adhere to a set schedule, making enforcing consistent screen time rules challenging.
- The family may resist hiring a caretaker because they believe there are enough people to care for the child.
- Space constraints may make keeping the child away from screens difficult, especially if a caretaker is present.
- Caretakers may receive conflicting instructions from different family members when parents are away.
- Older children may expose younger children to screen activities that parents wish to limit.
- To mitigate these challenges, consider the following strategies:
- If feasible, hire a caretaker to assist in managing screen time and explain to the family the benefits of having professional help.
- Guide the caretaker on engaging the child in screen-free activities and equip them with resources such as books and toys.

- Educate the family on the consequences of excessive screen time through a presentation emphasising the importance of parental control.
- Accept that complete control may not be possible and focus on minimising the negative impact of screen time.
- Communicate openly with family members about your decisions regarding screen time, explaining the rationale behind your choices.

You may have noticed that just as authoritative parents elucidate the reasons and consequences behind their rules to their children, it is equally important to communicate with your family members similarly. Effective communication plays a pivotal role in this context. By informing them about the reasons (the 'why'), the specific decisions you are making (the 'what'), and the strategies you plan to implement (the 'how'), you not only provide clarity to your family members but also gain clarity for yourself in the process. This transparent communication lets you explore creative approaches to reduce your child's screen time. The more actively engaged you are in this process, the more satisfaction and enjoyment you will derive from it.

Yes! Enjoying this journey despite all the challenges is crucial!

It is not sustainable if you start taking this as a painful task and do not enjoy it.

> **"If you are a parent seeking quick fixes without putting in additional effort, this book may not be suitable for you."**

Likewise, suppose you rely solely on external professionals such as doctors, teachers, or counsellors to manage your child's behaviour without actively participating. In that case, this book may not align with your approach. This book is designed for parents willing to invest time, effort, and active involvement in shaping their child's development, including their relationship with screens and technology.

# Chapter 8

# HANDLING PEER PRESSURE

When children are at home, it is a controlled environment. You can more or less control things.

But when they are with other children who are into screens, how do you manage them?

When fellow parents are not aware, how do you tackle that situation?

Your child might not be aware of the latest rhyme video channels, cartoon characters, reels, or shorts, and they might feel left out. How will you handle that?

We discussed the challenges parents might face while inculcating screen discipline. However, when we are trying to do that, your child might face an equal and opposing force in action.

**Peer pressure!**

Whenever I explain to parents the strategies to decrease their children's screen time, I am always asked these questions. You cannot control everything everywhere, but wherever you can, you have to try and minimise the damage, as I have mentioned before. I will give some basic guidelines on the most common scenarios to help you formulate your strategy based on your child's personality.

Children usually form friendships through various avenues-like society, school, extra-curricular activities, tuition, or daycare centres. Typically, a child interacts with a consistent group of friends. Consider this: if your child is mainly social, they have about 15 friends. Among these, 2-3 friends will significantly impact your child. As a responsible parent, sharing what you have learned from this book with these parents or encouraging them to read it themselves is crucial. Once they understand the consequences, implementing these guidelines can benefit all children. Imagine the impact when your child sees other kids following the same rules. They will not feel isolated. When home and social environments enforce similar rules, your child is likelier to adhere to them. Whenever children gather, ensure there's a screen-free space with engaging activities. Participate in their play to supervise and bond with them. Collaborating with other parents to plan and implement these activities will be incredibly rewarding. Working as a group or community yields excellent results. It is akin to group therapy, where everyone learns from each other's experiences. You can form online groups on social media platforms to share experiences and seek solutions.

If you are overwhelmed, focusing on educating 2-3 influential children's parents can still yield positive results. Children often imitate those closest to them. Ensuring these influential peers follow the same guidelines can positively influence your child.

Now, regarding keeping your child updated on the latest trends, utilise their limited co-watching screen time wisely. Choose content carefully, as not all trending material may suit your child. It will help if you stay updated on the latest trends to connect with your child and guide their screen time effectively. While you may fear that not exposing your child to technology early might hinder their future, rest assured that they are digital natives.

Consider this: even elderly individuals can easily navigate essential apps and websites despite never being exposed to technology in their earlier years. This is primarily due to app developers designing user-friendly interfaces catering to diverse demographics, from urban to rural settings and children to senior citizens. Your children, being digital natives, are naturally adept at technology. They are growing up in an era of rapid technological advancement, making it effortless to familiarise themselves with digital tools and platforms. There's no need for concern; they will likely learn to navigate technology faster than you did. Trust in their ability to adapt and thrive in the digital age.

We can mitigate the negative impacts of excessive screen time through these strategies. While we may not have complete control over every aspect, even small reductions in screen time can have significant benefits for your child and their friends.

# Chapter 9

# STEPS TO TAKE IF YOUR CHILD IS ALREADY DEPENDENT ON SCREENS

If you feel your child is dependent on the screen, assess the dependency on the EC-DUA scale given in the book. On the scale, if your child comes under moderate, high, or very high risk, you can try the following steps to help your child reduce screen dependency:

## 1) Collect Data and Facts

Start by becoming aware of your child's actual screen time. Just as a diet recall provides insight into your current eating habits when visiting a nutritionist, a screen time recall will give you an idea of your child's current screen time. Begin by tracking your child's screen time using screen time tracking apps or manually recording screen time for a few days. Be sure to include all devices your child uses, such as phones, tablets, computers, and TVs.

Here is a suggested format for manual tracking:

| Date and day | Time | Duration of usage | Device used | Type of usage |
|---|---|---|---|---|
| 03/08/24 Saturday | 9 am | 30 mins | iPad | YouTube videos |
|  |  |  |  |  |

| | | | | |
|---|---|---|---|---|
| | | | | |
| | | | | |
| | | | | |
| | | | | |

Understanding your child's screen usage specifics is crucial for devising an effective strategy. Here is how you can gain insight into your child's screen preferences and motivations:

- **Observe their screen activities:** Take note of what your child is doing on their device. Are they watching videos, playing games, or engaging in social media? Understanding their specific activities will help you tailor your approach accordingly.

- **Ask open-ended questions:** Encourage your child to share their interests and experiences with screen time. Ask questions like, "What do you enjoy doing on your tablet?" or "Why do you like watching those videos?" Answers to these questions will give you valuable insight into their motivations.

- **Engage in conversations:** Talk non-judgmentally with your child about screen usage. Listen actively to their responses and try to understand their perspective. This will help foster trust and open communication.

- **Monitor content:** Monitor the content your child is accessing online. Are they viewing age-appropriate content? Are there any concerning themes or behaviours? Understanding the content, they are drawn to will inform your strategy for managing screen time.

- **Identify motivations:** Determine what your child gets out of screen time. Is it entertainment, social interaction, learning, or something else? Understanding their motivations will help you address their needs and interests in healthier ways.

**If your child is too young and cannot speak, your observations will play a key role in collecting the information.**

By being aware of your child's specific screen activities and motivations, you can develop a targeted approach to managing their screen time and promoting healthier habits.

## 2) Identifying triggers

Pay attention to what prompts your child to use screens. Triggers can be external factors like notifications, time of day, presence of a particular person/friend, or internal factors like emotions such as boredom or frustration. Use the following categories to identify triggers:

| | |
|---|---|
| Emotional state | |
| People | |
| Places | |
| Things | |
| Time of the day | |
| Activities/situation | |
| Other | |

## 3) Devising a strategy

Based on identified triggers and the motivation behind using screens, create a plan to avoid or manage them effectively.

Here is how you can plan

a) **Replacing the habit:** Offer alternative activities to replace screen time. Create a timetable with various activity options and involve your child in the process. Replace screen time with alternative activities that will provide similar motivation. E.g. If your child is using the screen purely for entertainment purposes, the replacing activity should provide enough entertainment that he will not miss his screen.

b) **Take it slow and taper:** Gradually decrease screen time to avoid discomfort and withdrawal symptoms. Make small reductions in screen time over time.

c) **Involve children in decision-making:** If your child understands, include your child in setting screen time rules and boundaries. Explain the reasons behind these rules and offer rewards or incentives for positive behaviour.

d) **Lead by example and use the methods mentioned in the book:** Model healthy screen habits yourself by reducing your own screen time and engaging in alternative activities. Children mimic their parent's behaviour, so demonstrating balanced screen usage can encourage them to do the same.

By collecting data, identifying triggers, and devising a strategy, you can effectively help your child reduce screen dependency and develop healthier habits. Remember to be patient and supportive throughout the process.

# Chapter 10

# EARLY CHILDHOOD DEVICE USE ASSESSMENT (EC-DUA)

## Dr. Kruti Trivedi Abhyankar©

The Early Childhood Device Use Assessment (EC-DUA) is a comprehensive tool designed to help parents and caregivers evaluate and monitor young children's interaction with digital devices, aimed specifically at ages 2-5 years. In an increasingly digital world, where screens are omnipresent, EC-DUA serves as a vital resource to assess and manage digital device usage in early childhood.

**Assessment Process**

Parents or caregivers are instructed to observe and record their child's behaviors over the past month. They select the response that best reflects their child's typical interactions with digital devices. The assessment aims to provide a holistic view, considering both positive and potentially concerning behaviors associated with screen time.

**Scoring and Interpretation**

After completing the assessment, scores are tallied based on selected responses.

Each response corresponds to a score:

- □ 1$^{st}$ option = 0 points
- □ 2$^{nd}$ option = 1 point

- ☐ 3<sup>rd</sup> option = 2 points
- ☐ 4<sup>th</sup> Option = 3 points
- ☐ 5<sup>th</sup> Option = 4 points

Calculate the total score by summing up the scores for all questions.

A higher total score may indicate a greater risk of digital addiction or other associated issues. EC-DUA provides clear guidelines for interpreting these scores:

**Interpretation**

- **0-15 points:** Low risk of digital addiction. The child's digital device use appears to be within healthy limits, with minimal impact on various aspects of development and behavior.

- **16-30 points:** Moderate risk of digital addiction. There are indications that the child's digital device use may be starting to affect some aspects of their life, warranting closer monitoring and potential intervention to establish healthier habits.

- **31-45 points:** High risk of digital addiction. The child shows significant signs that digital device use is impacting various areas of their life, potentially indicating problematic behaviors and habits that require immediate attention and intervention.

- **46-60 points:** Very high risk of digital addiction. The child's digital device use is likely having a severe impact on their development, behavior, and daily life. Intensive intervention and support are recommended to address and mitigate the risks associated with digital addiction.

## Benefits and Outcomes

By using EC-DUA, parents gain valuable insights into their child's digital habits and their potential impact on development and well-being. It empowers parents to make informed decisions about managing screen time, fostering healthy behaviors, and promoting balanced activities essential for early childhood development.

## Instructions

Please answer the following questions based on your observations of your child's behavior over the past month. Select the option that best represents your child's typical behavior.

Child's Information:

Child's Name: _______________________________

Age: _______________________________

School: _______________________________


Parent's Information:

Parent's Name: _______________________________

Relationship to Child: _______________________________

Parent's Contact No. _______________________________

Parent's Email id _______________________________

Date: _______________________________

How would you rate your child's screen-time usage?

- ☐ Within healthy limits
- ☐ Slightly excessive
- ☐ Moderately excessive
- ☐ Very high

What type of content does your child mostly engage with on digital devices?

- ☐ Only Educational apps/games
- ☐ Mostly Educational apps/games
- ☐ Equal mix of Educational and Entertainment apps/games
- ☐ Mostly Entertainment apps/games
- ☐ Only Entertainment apps/games
- ☐ Other (please specify): ___________________

How often does your child use digital devices in the hour before bedtime?

- ☐ Never
- ☐ Rarely
- ☐ Sometimes
- ☐ Often
- ☐ Always

How often do you or another adult actively engage with your child during their digital device use?

- ☐ Never
- ☐ Rarely
- ☐ Sometimes
- ☐ Often
- ☐ Always

Do you use parental control apps or methods to manage your child's digital device usage and ensure age-appropriate content?

- ☐ Yes, actively use parental control apps or methods
- ☐ Yes, occasionally use parental control apps or methods
- ☐ No, do not use parental control apps or methods
- ☐ I don't know about such apps or methods, I don't use.

## Assessment Questions

### 1. Frequency of Digital Device Use

How often does your child use digital devices (e.g., tablets, smartphones, computers)?

- ☐ Never
- ☐ Rarely (less than 1 hour per day)
- ☐ Sometimes (1-2 hours per day)
- ☐ Often (3-4 hours per day)
- ☐ Always (more than 4 hours per day)

### 2. Increase in Screen-Time

Have you noticed a significant increase in your child's screen-time over the past few months?

- ☐ Not applicable
- ☐ No increase – Same screen-time
- ☐ Slight increase
- ☐ Moderate increase
- ☐ Significant increase

## 3. Physical Health

Have you noticed any physical health issues that might be related to digital device use (e.g., eye strain, headaches, reduced physical activity)?

- ☐ No issues
- ☐ Rarely
- ☐ Occasionally
- ☐ Often
- ☐ Always

## 4. Sleep Patterns

Has your child's sleep been affected by digital device use (e.g., difficulty falling asleep, waking up frequently)?

- ☐ Not affected
- ☐ Rarely (Once in 10-15 days)
- ☐ Occasionally (Once a week)
- ☐ Often (2-3 times a week)
- ☐ Always (>5 times a week)

## 5. Impact on Daily Activities

Has your child's use of digital devices interfered with their daily routines (e.g., meals, nap times, family activities)?

- ☐ Never
- ☐ Rarely
- ☐ Sometimes
- ☐ Often
- ☐ Always

## 6. Motor Developmental Delay

Have you noticed any delays in your child's motor skills development (e.g., fine motor skills, gross motor skills) that could be associated with excessive digital device use?

- ☐ Not Applicable
- ☐ May be but not sure
- ☐ Minor delays (slight delay in motor skills)
- ☐ Moderate delays (noticeable delay in motor skills)
- ☐ Severe delays (significant delay in motor skills)

## 7. Language Developmental Delay

Have you observed any delays in your child's language development (e.g., speech delay, vocabulary acquisition) that might be linked to screen-time habits?

- ☐ Not Applicable
- ☐ May be but not sure
- ☐ Minor delays (slight delay in motor skills)
- ☐ Moderate delays (noticeable delay in motor skills)
- ☐ Severe delays (significant delay in motor skills)

## 8. Communication and Eye Contact

How does your child communicate and maintain eye contact during interactions with others?

- ☐ Communicates well and maintains eye contact appropriately
- ☐ Occasionally has difficulty in communication or maintaining eye contact
- ☐ Frequently has difficulty in communication or maintaining eye contact

☐ Rarely communicates effectively or maintains eye contact

☐ Does not communicate effectively and avoids eye contact

## 9. Social Interaction

How has your child's digital device use affected their willingness to participate in physical or social play activities with other children?

☐ No impact, always willing to participate
☐ Minor impact, usually willing to participate
☐ Moderate impact, sometimes reluctant to participate
☐ Significant impact, often reluctant to participate
☐ Severe impact, rarely or never willing to participate

## 10. Attention Span and Concentration

How has digital device use affected your child's ability to concentrate on non-digital activities (e.g., playing with toys, listening to stories)?

☐ No impact, fully concentrates
☐ Minor impact, usually concentrates
☐ Moderate impact, sometimes has difficulty concentrating
☐ Significant impact, often has difficulty concentrating
☐ Severe impact, rarely or never concentrates

## 11. Emotional Responses

How does your child typically react when it's time to stop using digital devices?

☐ Calmly hands over the device

☐ Mildly resistant but eventually complies
☐ Becomes irritable or moody
☐ Cries or throws a tantrum
☐ Becomes extremely distressed or angry

## 12. Behavioral Responses

How does your child react when unable to use digital devices when desired?

☐ Not Applicable
☐ Accepts the refusal easily if diverted
☐ Asks persistently but accepts refusal
☐ Becomes irritable or moody
☐ Throws tantrums or exhibits aggressive behavior

## 13. Lying or Hiding Behaviors

Have you noticed your child engaging in lying or hiding behaviors related to their screen-time usage?

☐ Never
☐ Rarely
☐ Sometimes
☐ Often
☐ Always

## 14. Aggression or Behavioral Issues

Have you noticed an increase in aggression or other behavioral issues coinciding with your child's screen-time?

☐ No Issues
☐ Rarely
☐ Sometimes (occasional aggression or behavioral issues)

- ☐ Often (frequent aggression or behavioral issues)
- ☐ Severe issues (chronic aggression or behavioral issues)

## 15. Adherence to Screen-Time Limits

How does your child respond to attempts at limiting their screen-time?

- ☐ Always adheres to limits set without issue
- ☐ Usually adheres to limits but occasionally asks for more time
- ☐ Sometimes adheres to limits but often asks for more time
- ☐ Rarely adheres to limits and frequently asks for more time
- ☐ Never adheres to limits and always asks for more time

# Chapter 11

# INTERNET ADDICTION TEST FOR ADULTS

So, this questionnaire is for you.

**Assess yourself on this scale.**

This questionnaire consists of 20 statements. After reading each statement carefully, based upon the 5-point Likert scale, please select the response (0, 1, 2, 3, 4 or 5) which best describes you. If two choices seem to apply equally well, circle the choice that best represents how you are most of the time during the past month. Be sure to read all the statements carefully before making your choice. The statements refer to offline situations or actions unless otherwise specified.

0 = Not Applicable **1** = Rarely **2** = Occasionally **3** = Frequently **4** = Often **5** = Always

1. How often do you find that you stay online longer than you intended?
2. How often do you neglect household chores to spend more time online?
3. How often do you prefer the excitement of the Internet to intimacy with your partner?
4. How often do you form new relationships with fellow online users?

5.  How often do others in your life complain to you about the amount of time you spend online?

6.  How often do your grades or school work suffer because of the amount of time you spend online?

7.  How often do you check your email before something else that you need to do?

8.  How often does your job performance or productivity suffer because of the Internet?

9.  How often do you become defensive or secretive when anyone asks you what you do online?

10.  How often do you block out disturbing thoughts about your life with soothing thoughts of the Internet?

11.  How often do you find yourself anticipating when you will go online again?

12.  How often do you fear that life without the Internet would be boring, empty, and joyless?

13.  How often do you snap, yell, or act annoyed if someone bothers you while you are online?

14.  How often do you lose sleep due to being online?

15.  How often do you feel preoccupied with the Internet when off-line, or fantasize about being online?

16.  How often do you find yourself saying "just a few more minutes" when online?

17.  How often do you try to cut down the amount of time you spend online and fail?

18.  How often do you try to hide how long you've been online?

19.  How often do you choose to spend more time online over going out with others?

20.  How often do you feel depressed, moody, or nervous when you are off-line, which goes away once you are back online?

## Scoring Guidelines

The IAT total score is the sum of the ratings given by the examinee for the 20 item responses. Each item is rated on a 5-point scale ranging from 0 to 5. The maximum score is 100 points.

The IAT total score ranges, with the higher the score representing the higher level of severity of Internet compulsivity and addiction. Total scores that range from 0 to 30 points are considered to reflect a normal level of Internet usage; scores of 31 to 49 indicate the presence of a mild level of Internet addiction; 50 to 79 reflect the presence of a moderate level; and scores of 80 to 100 indicate a severe dependence upon the Internet. Research addressing the sensitivity and validity of these score ranges is published in several journals. The IAT is validated in several languages so the examiner should review the correct study based on the language used for administration.

The examiner should evaluate the score ranges for the purposes for which the IAT is being used. If the examiner's purpose is to measure detection of persons with Internet addiction, then the upper level of each range should be lowered to minimize false negatives. This method would be useful in screening for possible cases of Internet addiction. To reduce the number of false positives, the examiner should raise the upper level of each range. This method is used in research for which one wishes to obtain as pure a sample as possible of persons with Internet addiction.

# Chapter 12

# CULTIVATING BALANCE FOR A DIGITAL FUTURE

As we conclude this journey through the landscape of digital well-being for young children, it's clear that our role as parents and caregivers has never been more critical. Technology will continue to evolve, becoming an even more integral part of our daily lives, but it's up to us to guide our children in developing healthy, balanced relationships with the digital world.

By understanding the effects of screen-time on development, identifying signs of digital dependency, and fostering habits of self-regulation and mindfulness, we are laying the groundwork for their future success—not just in a digital sense, but in all aspects of life. The seeds of discipline and awareness we plant today will shape the way our children interact with technology for years to come.

The journey of raising mindful digital natives is ongoing. It requires patience, intention, and continuous learning, but the reward is immeasurable—a generation of children who can navigate technology with confidence, without losing their connection to the real world.

As we move forward, let's remember that

*"Balance is the key."*

By cultivating environments where both screen-time and real-world experiences coexist harmoniously, we're giving our children the tools to thrive in a future filled with limitless possibilities. The responsibility is ours, but the impact is theirs—for a lifetime.

All the best on your parenting journey in raising digital natives!

# SUMMARY TABLES

## Effects of excessive screen-time

| Aspects | Summary |
| --- | --- |
| Language and Motor Development | Two studies conducted India, highlighted the significant association between increased screen time and developmental delay, particularly affecting language acquisition and communication skills. |
| Emotional and Social Development | Excessive screen time impedes children's ability to read faces and learn social skills crucial for developing empathy. Lack of human interaction during screen time affects babies' communication and emotional development. |
| Cognitive Development | Higher screen time among preschool children is associated with suspected cognitive delays, as it detracts from activities that stimulate cognitive development and boost brainpower, such as play and interaction with peers. |
| Learning | Infants under a year old do not effectively learn from screens, emphasizing the importance of human interaction for meaningful learning experiences. |

| Aspects | Summary |
| --- | --- |
| Sleep | Excessive screen time, especially exposure to blue light emitted by screens, disrupts sleep patterns by suppressing melatonin production and interfering with circadian rhythms. This disruption can lead to difficulty falling asleep, delayed sleep onset, and daytime drowsiness. |
| Childhood Obesity | Excessive screen time is linked to childhood obesity through mechanisms such as reduced physical activity, increased snacking, exposure to food advertisements, and disrupted sleep patterns. Interventions aimed at reducing screen time have shown promising results in improving sleep duration, behavior, sociability, academic performance, and weight management. |
| Attention Span | Excessive screen time, particularly for children under five, has been linked to attention deficit hyperactivity disorder (ADHD) and other focus-related issues. Screen-based activities provide immediate and repeated stimulation, which may hinder the development and utilization of directed attention required for tasks like studying or reading. |

| Aspects | Summary |
| --- | --- |
| Impulse Control | Prolonged screen exposure can lead to alterations in dopamine levels in the brain, similar to the effects of addictive substances like cocaine. This can result in difficulties in impulse control, manifested as challenges in delaying gratification and managing screen time usage. |
| Physical Health | Excessive screen time is associated with various physical health issues, including digital eyestrain, hearing problems, neck and back pains, and repetitive strain injuries (RSIs) such as tendonitis and carpal tunnel syndrome. Moreover, poor posture and reduced physical activity due to screen use can lead to spinal health issues and musculoskeletal problems in children. |
| Brain Changes due to Screens | Prolonged screen exposure can lead to structural and functional changes in the brain, affecting areas associated with learning, attention, decision-making, and emotional regulation. These changes include alterations in white matter integrity, disruptions in neural connectivity, and abnormal activation patterns in regions implicated in emotional processing and impulse control. Concerns about the impact of cell phone radiation on children's developing brains and bodies have also been raised. |

| Aspects | Summary |
|---|---|
| Effect of Radiation | Children are more susceptible to RF radiation due to their smaller heads and brains compared to adults. Research has suggested a correlation between early cell phone use and an increased risk of developing brain tumors, especially among individuals who start using wireless phones before the age of 20. Studies have also explored the potential impact of cell phone exposure on children's behavior, indicating a heightened risk of developing behavioral problems, including hyperactivity and difficulties in social interaction. |

## Ideal Screen-time limits

| Age group | Guidelines |
|---|---|
| Less than 2 years old | Completely avoid screen use |
| 2 to 5 years old | • Introduce digital media content only under parental or adult guidance and monitoring.<br>• Limit viewing to specific purposes such as educational games or teaching aids.<br>• Viewing should not exceed 30 minutes per session and no more than two sessions per day.<br>• Adult interaction during media use is crucial.<br>• Avoid fast-paced programs, apps with distracting content, and any violent content. |

## Parental habits that can lead to a possibility of increased screen-time in children

| Scenario | Impact on child | Recommendations |
|---|---|---|
| Giving screens during meal time | • Distraction from feeling physiologic satiety.<br>• Habituation to mindless eating and overeating.<br>• Increased risk of childhood obesity.<br>• Reduced enjoyment of food.<br>• Decreased awareness of food intake.<br>• Potential memory issues regarding consumed meals. | • Completely avoid screen use during meal times.<br>• Encourage mindful eating practices without digital distractions. |
| Using gadgets as pacifiers when they are bored or upset | • Hinders creativity development.<br>• Encourages dependency on technology for emotional regulation.<br>• Impairs communication skills and emotional awareness.<br>• Leads to disengagement with real-world interactions.<br>• Diminished parent-child bonding. | • Encourage alternative activities to overcome boredom, such as creative play or outdoor exploration.<br>• Provide emotional support and validation rather than relying solely on digital pacifiers.<br>• Model healthy emotional coping mechanisms. |

| Scenario | Impact on child | Recommendations |
|---|---|---|
| | • Creates reliance on digital platforms to soothe negative emotions.<br>• Limits opportunities for healthy emotional expression and coping strategies. | |
| Using gadgets in front of your child even when you are not working | • Sets inconsistent role modelling for screen use.<br>• Reinforces unhealthy screen habits.<br>• Missed opportunities for parent-child bonding.<br>• Limits exposure to alternative recreational activities.<br>• Fosters dependence on screens for leisure and relaxation.<br>• Diminishes parent-child interactions and communication.<br>• Contradiction between parental guidance and actions. May lead to excessive screen time in children. | • Establish dedicated screen-free times for bonding and recreational activities.<br>• Engage in shared activities that do not involve screens.<br>• Set clear boundaries and adhere to them consistently.<br>• Be mindful of your own screen usage in front of your child. |

| Scenario | Impact on child | Recommendations |
|---|---|---|
| Phubbing: Looking at a screen and not paying attention while your child is trying to communicate with you | • Conveys disregard for child's communication. - Undermines the importance of child's thoughts and feelings.<br>• Discourages open and meaningful communication.<br>• Diminishes parent-child connection and trust.<br>• Sets a precedent for inattentive communication habits.<br>• May lead to feelings of neglect or resentment in the child.<br>• Encourages disengagement from family interactions.<br>• Hinders development of effective communication skills.<br>• Erodes parent-child relationship. | • Prioritize active listening and engagement during conversations.<br>• Establish clear communication boundaries regarding device usage.<br>• Model attentive and respectful communication behaviors.<br>• Allocate dedicated quality time for uninterrupted interactions with your child.<br>• Create a technology-free zone during family discussions and bonding activities. |

| Scenario | Impact on child | Recommendations |
| --- | --- | --- |
| Giving a gadget to your child for personal peace | • Encourages dependency on screens for entertainment.<br>• Normalizes unhealthy screen habits.<br>• Increases risk of digital addiction.<br>• Hinders development of independent play skills.<br>• Limits opportunities for imaginative and creative activities.<br>• May lead to excessive screen time and sedentary behaviour.<br>• Diminishes parental involvement and supervision.<br>• Undermines child's self-regulation and autonomy.<br>• Impedes healthy emotional regulation and coping strategies. | • Seek alternative strategies for personal relaxation and rejuvenation.<br>• Encourage independent play and exploration without screens.<br>• Set boundaries on screen use and adhere to them consistently.<br>• Provide opportunities for imaginative and creative play.<br>• Foster autonomy and self-directed activities.<br>• Model healthy coping mechanisms and stress management strategies. |
| Not saying NO when they ask for your phone or any gadget from you | • Reinforces the perception that screen use is permissible at all times. | • Establish clear boundaries and expectations regarding screen access. |

| Scenario | Impact on child | Recommendations |
| --- | --- | --- |
|  | • Encourages manipulation and dependency on screens.<br>• Fosters a sense of entitlement regarding device access.<br>• May lead to excessive screen time and dependence.<br>• Undermines parental authority and consistency.<br>• Compromises efforts to establish screen use guidelines.<br>• Hinders development of self-regulation and delayed gratification.<br>• Sets unrealistic expectations for device availability. | • Consistently enforce screen time guidelines and limits.<br>• Encourage alternative activities and diversions.<br>• Teach children the importance of delayed gratification and self-control.<br>• Model assertive and consistent communication.<br>• Offer explanations for limitations and reinforce boundaries with positive reinforcement. |
| Praising them regarding their screen use in front of other people | • Reinforces undesired behaviour and screen dependency.<br>• Normalizes excessive screen time in social settings.<br>• Encourages continued engagement in screen activities for validation. | • Refrain from praising screen use as an achievement or desirable behavior.<br>• Redirect praise towards alternative activities and accomplishments.<br>• Model and reinforce behaviors aligned with healthy screen habits. |

| Scenario | Impact on child | Recommendations |
| --- | --- | --- |
| | • May lead to parental reinforcement of unhealthy screen habits.<br>• Hinders efforts to promote balanced screen use.<br>• Fosters a sense of accomplishment and pride in screen use.<br>• Creates unrealistic expectations for screen-based achievements.<br>• Impedes efforts to establish screen time boundaries. | • Educate others about the importance of balanced screen use in children.<br>• Focus on praising non-screen-related achievements and positive behaviors.<br>• Reinforce the value of diverse interests and activities beyond screens. |
| Giving them gadgets without monitoring or co-watching | • Exposes children to potentially harmful or inappropriate content.<br>• Undermines parental oversight and supervision.<br>• Reinforces lack of accountability and responsibility. | |

## How to sow the seeds of screen discipline for your child?

| Scenario | Impact on child | Recommendations |
|---|---|---|
| Set a routine for your child and establish a fixed time for co-watching screens. | • Promotes consistency and predictability in screen time.<br>• Facilitates adherence to screen time limits.<br>• Encourages self-regulation and time management skills.<br>• Reduces resistance to screen time restrictions. | • Incorporate screen time into the child's daily routine with a designated time slot.<br>• Emphasize the importance of following the schedule for screen time. - Ensure other activities are also included in the routine for balanced development. |
| Plan your child's screen time in advance and establish a purpose for co-watching. | • Increases engagement and excitement for screen time.<br>• Enables focused and purposeful media consumption.<br>• Facilitates parental guidance and discussion.<br>• Supports intentional learning and skill development. | • Determine specific goals or themes for each screen time session.<br>• Create a weekly schedule of planned activities and content.<br>• Involve the child in selecting educational or entertaining programs.<br>• Discuss the objectives and outcomes of each screen time session with the child. |

| Scenario | Impact on child | Recommendations |
| --- | --- | --- |
| Discuss while co-watching screens | • Enhances communication and bonding between parent and child.<br>• Encourages critical thinking and reflection.<br>• Fosters a deeper understanding of media content.<br>• Promotes active participation and engagement. | • Pause periodically to discuss observations, thoughts, and feelings about the content.<br>• Encourage open-ended questions and active listening.<br>• Provide constructive feedback and share personal perspectives.<br>• Create a supportive and non-judgmental environment for sharing opinions.<br>• Incorporate learning objectives or challenges to stimulate discussion and interaction. |
| Establish screen-free family fun time | • Strengthens family relationships and cohesion.<br>• Encourages alternative forms of entertainment and bonding.<br>• Promotes creativity and imagination. | • Allocate dedicated time for family activities without screens.<br>• Plan a variety of engaging and enjoyable activities for all family members. |

| Scenario | Impact on child | Recommendations |
| --- | --- | --- |
| | • Provides opportunities for shared experiences and memories. | • Designate specific areas in the home as technology-free zones during family time.<br>• Rotate leadership roles for selecting and organizing screen-free activities.<br>• Emphasize the importance of quality time spent together as a family. |
| Utilize weekends for meaningful parent-child interactions and outdoor activities. | • Enhances parent-child bonding and attachment.<br>• Facilitates exploration and discovery.<br>• Promotes physical activity and healthy lifestyles.<br>• Fosters shared experiences and memories. | • Reserve weekends for special outings, adventures, or leisure activities.<br>• Prioritize quality time spent with your child over work or personal tasks.<br>• Incorporate outdoor adventures, nature walks, or cultural experiences into weekend plans. |

| Scenario | Impact on child | Recommendations |
|---|---|---|
| | | • Limit screen time during weekends to promote face-to-face interactions and active engagement.<br>• Capture and cherish memorable moments through photographs or journals. |
| Introduce your child to different emotions and emotional literacy skills. | • Develops emotional awareness and vocabulary.<br>• Enhances self-regulation and coping abilities.<br>• Facilitates healthy expression and understanding of emotions.<br>• Promotes empathy and social skills. | • Teach children basic emotions through pictures, stories, and real-life examples.<br>• Encourage verbal expression of emotions and feelings in everyday situations.<br>• Introduce the concept of "feeling fingerprints" to help children recognize physical cues associated with different emotions.<br>• Incorporate emotional vocabulary into daily conversations and interactions. |

| Scenario | Impact on child | Recommendations |
| --- | --- | --- |
| | | • Model positive emotional behaviours and coping strategies for children to emulate.<br>• Foster a supportive and empathetic environment for emotional exploration and expression. |
| Children learn from you | • Parental modeling influences children's behavior and attitudes.<br>• Children observe and imitate parental actions and decisions.<br>- Parental behavior shapes children's values and habits.<br>- Consistent role modeling fosters healthy habits and behaviors in children. | • Demonstrate responsible technology use by prioritizing tasks and delaying gratification in front of your child.<br>- Highlight the importance of fulfilling obligations before indulging in leisure activities.<br>- Communicate openly about the decision-making process to reinforce the rationale behind prioritization. |

| Scenario | Impact on child | Recommendations |
|---|---|---|
| | | - Encourage delayed gratification by setting realistic expectations and honoring commitments.<br>- Emphasize the value of patience and self-discipline in achieving desired outcomes. |
| Delay the craving/impulse | • Teaches children impulse control and self-regulation skills. - Empowers children to manage their impulses and cravings effectively. - Promotes mindful decision-making and goal-directed behavior. - Reduces impulsive and compulsive behaviors related to screen use. | • Teach children the 4D method: Delay, Distract, Deep breathing, Drink water.<br>- Practice delaying gratification by postponing screen time or cravings for a set period.<br>- Encourage alternative activities to distract from cravings, such as physical exercises, creative hobbies, or mindfulness techniques. |

| Scenario | Impact on child | Recommendations |
|---|---|---|
| | | - Promote deep breathing and relaxation exercises as coping strategies for managing impulses.<br>- Model and reinforce the use of these techniques during challenging situations. |
| Communicating openly | • Establishes trust and openness in parent-child relationships.<br>- Encourages children to seek guidance and support when faced with online challenges. - Empowers children to navigate digital environments safely and responsibly.<br>- Facilitates early intervention and prevention of cyberbullying or online risks. | • Foster a non-judgmental and supportive environment for open communication about technology use. - Initiate regular discussions about online experiences, concerns, and questions.<br>- Provide age-appropriate guidance on digital safety, privacy, and responsible online behavior. - Empower children to report any uncomfortable or harmful encounters online without fear of punishment. |

| Scenario | Impact on child | Recommendations |
|---|---|---|
|  |  | - Stay informed about current trends and issues in digital media to address evolving challenges effectively. |
| Communicating about problematic and healthier usage of technology | • Raises awareness of the distinction between healthy and problematic screen use. - Encourages critical thinking and discernment in evaluating digital content and activities. - Empowers children to make informed choices about their screen time habits. - Promotes responsible and mindful technology use from a young age. | • Discuss the concept of "Digital Candy" (problematic screen exposure) versus "Digital Vegetables" (healthier screen usage) with your child. - Explain the potential risks and benefits associated with different types of screen activities. - Encourage reflection on personal screen habits and preferences to identify areas for improvement. - Model balanced and purposeful screen use in front of your child to reinforce positive behaviors. |

| Scenario | Impact on child | Recommendations |
| --- | --- | --- |
| | | - Incorporate discussions about digital literacy and media literacy into everyday conversations to promote critical thinking skills. |
| Storytelling | • Engages children's imagination and creativity. - Communicates complex concepts and values in a relatable and accessible manner. - Captures children's attention and interest through narrative storytelling. - Reinforces learning and behavioral messages through storytelling experiences. | • Create or select stories that illustrate the importance of screen discipline and responsible technology use. - Use storytelling as a tool to discuss the consequences of excessive screen time and the benefits of balanced media consumption. - Incorporate characters and scenarios that resonate with your child's experiences and interests. - Encourage active participation by asking questions, eliciting reactions, and inviting discussions after storytelling sessions. |

| Scenario | Impact on child | Recommendations |
| --- | --- | --- |
|  |  | - Make storytelling a regular part of family routines to reinforce positive messages and foster communication around screen-related topics. |

## Parenting Styles

| Parenting Style | Description | Impact on children |
| --- | --- | --- |
| Authoritative Parenting | • Balanced approach with high demands and high warmth.<br>• Encourages open communication and rational discussions.<br>• Listens to the child's perspective and provides guidance with clear rules and reasonable expectations.<br>• Empathetic, emotionally intelligent, and responsive to the child's needs.<br>• Enforces discipline positively, considering individual interests and explaining consequences. | • Happy and emotionally intelligent children.<br>• Independent and academically successful.<br>• Possess strong social skills.<br>• Fewer mental health issues or addictions. |

| Parenting Style | Description | Impact on children |
| --- | --- | --- |
| Authoritarian Parenting | • High demands but low warmth.<br>• Strict rules enforced with harsh punishments.<br>• High expectations with minimal explanation or flexibility.<br>• Critical and imposing rigid rules.<br>• Little emotional support or warmth shown. | • More likely to experience mental health issues.<br>• Lower self-esteem and struggle with independence.<br>• Poor emotional intelligence and academic performance.<br>• Limited social skills and higher susceptibility to addictions. |
| Permissive/ Indulgent Parenting | • Low demands but high warmth.<br>• Non-punitive and accepting approach with abundant freedom.<br>• Complete autonomy for children with minimal responsibility.<br>• Prioritizes warmth and love, sometimes resorting to material rewards.<br>• Acts more like friends than authoritative figures. | • Less happy children with lack of respect for authority.<br>• Struggle with self-control and rule-breaking behavior.<br>• Challenges in social settings and poor emotional regulation.<br>• Experience poor mental health and lack of emotional regulation. |

| Parenting Style | Description | Impact on children |
| --- | --- | --- |
| Neglectful/ Uninvolved Parenting | • Low demands and low warmth.<br>• Minimal involvement in children's lives with little interest, affection, or emotional support.<br>• Children raise themselves with minimal guidance or structure.<br>• Little time spent with children and minimal expectations. | • Poor mental health and low self-esteem.<br>• Anxiety, stress, and difficulty coping with emotions.<br>• Higher susceptibility to addictions and engagement in criminal behavior as adolescents.<br>• Struggle academically due to lack of parental involvement and support. |

## Parenting styles in Screen-discipline context

| Parenting Style | Description | Impact on children |
| --- | --- | --- |
| Authoritative Parenting | • Establishes clear rules and screen-time limits.<br>• Provides essential knowledge on digital literacy and online threats.<br>• Maintains open communication and stays informed about technology. | • Children develop healthy internet habits with understanding of digital literacy and online safety.<br>• Balanced use of technology with parental oversight.<br>• Reduced risk of internet addiction and exposure to online threats. |

| Parenting Style | Description | Impact on children |
|---|---|---|
| | • Exercises control with balanced boundaries. | • Fosters positive parent-child relationships through dialogue and care. |
| Authoritarian Parenting | • Imposes strict rules and demands obedience without explanation.<br>• Punishment is used for non-compliance.<br>• Communication tends to be one-sided, favouring the parent's directives. | • Children may develop fear or resentment towards authority.<br>• Lack of understanding of internet safety and healthy technology use.<br>• Potential for unhealthy internet behaviour and addiction due to lack of dialogue and explanation.<br>• Limited opportunity for children to develop critical thinking skills or make informed decisions about their online activities. |
| Permissive/ Indulgent Parenting | • Prioritizes children's needs and maintains open communication. | • Children may develop excessive internet habits without limits or supervision. |

| Parenting Style | Description | Impact on children |
| --- | --- | --- |
| | • Fails to establish firm rules or boundaries.<br>• Children dictate terms, often granted unrestricted internet access. | • Lack of structure may lead to difficulties in self-regulation and time management.<br>• Increased risk of exposure to online dangers and inappropriate content.<br>• Dependency on technology for entertainment or validation. |
| Neglectful/ Uninvolved Parenting | • Exhibits minimal involvement and fails to provide love, communication, or guidance.<br>• Sets no rules or limits regarding internet usage. | • Children lack guidance on internet safety and responsible technology use.<br>• Vulnerable to the negative effects of unrestricted internet access, such as exposure to inappropriate content or online predators.<br>• Increased risk of developing unhealthy internet habits or addiction. |

| Parenting Style | Description | Impact on children |
|---|---|---|
| | | • Lack of parental support or oversight may lead to feelings of neglect or isolation.<br>• Impaired development of critical thinking skills and inability to navigate online challenges effectively. |